The King's Riches

Words of encouragement to enrich the soul.

Tamarah West

Mona,
You are amazing! Thankyou for your love & encouragement!
Enjoy!
Tamarah!

How to Use This Book

This book was designed with the freedom to read at random. You can embark on a treasure hunt of sorts. The riches of wisdom, encouragement and insight are found as you open the book to explore the treasures hidden all around. I would encourage you to gather a journal as you take this journey. Reflect and record what God reveals to you. Perhaps that is the truest treasure of all, that God reveals Himself to us. Have fun and happy treasuring!

Dedication

This book would not be possible without the love and encouragement of countless gems of people I have had the privilege of knowing. Each one adds a depth and clarity that truly makes me rich. May the love and encouragement you show me be multiplied back to you a thousand-fold.

"But grow in the grace and knowledge of our Lord
and Savior Jesus Christ. To him be glory both
now and forever! Amen."
2 Peter 3:18, NIV

Grace and Favor

"My heart rejoices to see your face. You are My lovely one, full
of grace. My favor rests on you. Release it in faith. I have given
you all you need and then some. I am a generous God who
takes care of your every need. I give you bread to eat and seed
to sow. Plant it in faith and watch it grow. Believe and see as I
believe and see. You have My mind, My words, and My heart.
Release My joy. The gifts I give are for you to impart."

"Praise be to the Lord my Rock, who trains my hands for war, my fingers for battle."
Psalm 144:1, NIV

Qualified and Skilled

"You are My qualified one. I have given and will continue to give you the skills you need to do what I have called you to do. We do this together. You and Me, hand in hand. Lean on Me and learn from Me. I will teach the hungry soul. You are not half. You are whole. I will complete the work I have begun. I am the Victor, and the battle, I have won."

*"And hope does not put us to shame, because
God's love has been poured out into our hearts
through the Holy Spirit, who has been given
to us."*
Romans 5:5, NIV

Seeds of Hope

"Renew the hope I have placed inside. You are made to shine, not hide. I have made you bold with strength in your soul. See yourself as I see you: complete and whole. You are the one I need. I have given you the seed. Plant My words of strength, encouragement, and hope. I will show you the fields to sow. Trust Me. Plant and watch the harvest grow. Growth comes from your obedience. Seek and see. See and do. Know that I am always for you."

"But we have this treasure in jars of clay to show that this all-surpassing power is from God and not from us."

2 Corinthians 4:7, NIV

Eyes to See

"I have declared the end from the beginning. I can see what you cannot. I have more for you than you can think or imagine. Starve your doubts by feeding your faith. I have many and mighty plans for you. You are not without direction. You are divinely guided by Me. Allow Me to lead you to things unseen. Hope springing forth and joy overflowing. I have given you tools and skills. Use what I have given you and you will get more. Share Me with others and allow My influence to grow. Look and see who I will lead you to for you to bless. Eyes on Me and you will see. May your mind and heart of Christ be open to give and receive. Choose to rejoice. Choose to believe."

"...they will break through the gate and go out.
Their King will pass through before them, the
Lord at their head."

Micah 2:13, NIV

Follow the Breaker

"I have gone up with a shout. I am your Breaker and I have
broken forth. Follow Me. I will show you the way. Forward
motion is not so slippery if you walk in the path I have laid
out for you. I have put My Spirit in you to lead and guard and
guide. He is your strength when you want to hide. I have made
you bold with strength in your soul. Be not afraid to make a
goal. I have given you the wisdom that you asked for. Ask again,
should you need more."

"Enlarge the place of your tent, stretch your tent curtains wide, do not hold back; lengthen your cords, strengthen your stakes."
Isaiah 54:2, NIV

Broaden Your Borders

"Get ready for the more I have for you. Expand your borders. Lengthen your vision beyond the limitations you have placed on it. I will cause you to see beyond what you have seen before. To believe what you have not believed before. I am the One who guides you into truth. I am the One who renews your youth. I have given you much more than you can think or imagine. I will increase your capacity for more. Thank Me for what I have done, am doing, and will continue to do on your behalf. I am the God of abundance, not lack. You will see each word is a seed. Each expectation is the soil. I will more than meet the need. Rejoice this day in the joy that I give. Be free this day. Have fun and live."

"Each of you should use whatever gift you have received to serve others, as faithful stewards of God's grace in its various forms."
1 Peter 4:10, NIV

Give the Gifts I Have Given

"I have given you My word. You have hidden it in your heart. You know the truth that we will never part. We are bonded in love. Nothing can separate. I have called you to love yourself, not berate yourself. See yourself through My eyes. Love you as I love you. You are a winner, not a loser. You are a success, not a failure. I have given you abilities you have not begun to recognize. Ask Me to show you how to bring them forth. The world is waiting for you to recover the gifts you did not know you had."

*"For we are God's handiwork, created in Christ
Jesus to do good works, which God prepared in
advance for us to do."*
Ephesians 2:10, NIV

Crafted to Create

"I deliver you and I will deliver you of that which no longer serves you. Be open to Me and new and renewed ways of thinking and behaving. I reveal to you the truth you need to make your own. I will give you exactly what you need for life and life abundantly. Trust Me to give you what you think you lack. Trust Me to know I have your back. You are My wondrous work that shall declare that My name is near. You are My workmanship created for good works in Me. Your purpose was crafted into your creation."

"Your eyes saw my unformed body; all the days ordained for me were written in your book before one of them came to be."
Psalm 139:16, NIV

Planned on Purpose

"You are My chosen one; created on purpose and by design. You were not made to be put on a shelf and gather dust. You were made to have an impact on those who encounter you. You will have insights and words that will make them think, and draw them to Me. You were created to impact and interact with others. You live in a rhythm of divine appointments. Dance in the divine. You are called to shine. Just as I awaken the dawn, I will awaken you. There is work to be done. Hearts and lives that need healed. No longer shall you be concealed in doubt and fear. I will show you that I am near."

*"And we all, who with unveiled faces contemplate
the Lord's glory, are being transformed into his
image with ever- increasing glory, which comes
from the Lord, who is the Spirit."*
2 CorinthianS 3:18, NIV

Revelation Transforms

"I reveal Myself to you. I reveal yourself to you. You shall see yourself and others through the lens of My love. My love covers your imperfections, because you are made complete in Me. There is no lack in My kingdom. Bring this truth into your day to day, and be an example and an inspiration for others. There is more than enough, you are more than enough, and you have dominion. You have a responsibility to share what you have and know with others, so they can be transformed as well. Revelation applied is transformation personified."

*"Come, all you who are thirsty, come to the
waters; and you who have no money, come,
buy and eat! Come, buy wine and milk without
money and without cost."*
Isaiah 55:1, NIV

Drink Freely

"Grace and peace be multiplied to you. When you feel you have
nothing to give, come to Me and drink freely of My unending
supply. Show others the joy of knowing Me; the exuberance
of knowing who you are in Me. Show them the love and
protection of knowing what concerns you, concerns me, too. I
am your advocate. You are My ambassador. I give you authority
and wisdom to rule as I rule, because we belong to each other.
What you think you lack can be found in Me. The supply is
plentiful. Know this to be true: all these riches do not compare
with spending time with you."

"The angel of the Lord encamps around those who fear him, and he delivers them."
Psalm 34:7, NIV

Protected for a Purpose

"I am the glory in your midst. I am the One who drives out your enemies and secures your borders. I am the one who decided to take stock in you, to believe in you. I do not regret My decision. I am your glory and the lifter of your head. Look up and see. Declare what I have said. There are more for you than against you. You belong to Me and I protect that which is Mine. You are My hope-filled one, meant to shine."

"Whether you turn to the right or to the left, your ears will hear a voice behind you, saying, "This is the way; walk in it."
Isaiah 30:21, NIV

Directional Challenge

"Go forth in the direction I will show you. You can do all I have called you to do. I am calling you higher. I am calling you into the new. Great and mighty are the plans I have laid out. Arise and go forth with a shout. Today is the day I call you to walk with Me. Speak as I speak and see as I see."

"Before I formed you in the womb I knew you,
before you were born I set you apart; I appointed
you as a prophet to the nations."
Jeremiah 1:5, NIV

Called and Qualified

"I am the Light that enlightens your darkness. I am the Hope that dispels despair. I am the Truth that extinguishes the lie. You are My ambassador. You emulate Me and speak My directives. You are the compass to those who lack direction. You are the glasses for those who lack vision. You will teach them what you know, what I will show. Your qualification is found in Me. I have called you to arise, that I may shine. Step into that which I have for you. It is only as difficult as a choice. Choose to do so. Choose to arise and let Me shine in you and through you. It is Me in you that is the hope of glory. Take part in the awesomeness of your story."

*"He lifted me out of the slimy pit, out of the mud
and mire; he set my feet on a rock and gave me a
firm place to stand."*
Psalm 40:2, NIV

Trust your Foundation

"I have called you up out of the pit and I have placed you on the rock. I am your firm foundation. I have given you a solid, firm footing. You will grow and gain confidence as you learn to trust in Me, and trust that My heart is for you. I call you forth to take you higher. The higher you go with Me, the greater and broader perspective you will have. See the big picture, but also take part in the smaller details. Seek Me for the proper perspective. I will align your vision to Mine. I am the Light that causes you to shine."

*"The plans of the diligent lead to profit as surely
as haste leads to poverty."*
Proverbs 21:5, NIV

Fruit of Faithfulness

"I have given you My promise. I have given you My word. I will watch over My word to perform it. I bring about the result as you till the ground of faith. I will bring you fruit in due season if you do not give up. Success follows consistency. You can trust fully in Me. I will show you the way to go. I will show you which seeds to sow. I am the Lord of the harvest. The One who multiplies and increases whatever you give to Me. I give you gifts for the good of you and others. Share freely that which you have freely received."

"Deep calls to deep in the roar of your waterfalls;
all your waves and breakers have swept
over me."
Psalm 42:7, NIV

Drawn to the Deep

"I am the One who sees the best in you and draws you forth.
When you believe in the beauty of you, your life and the lives
of those around you will be transformed. Those who know
the value of water will draw from the well. I am the One who
causes the abundance of the sea to be drawn to you. Deep calls
unto deep at the mention of My name. When you give Me
permission to transform you, you will never be the same. I am
He who goes before and prepares the way. I am the One who
will forever stay."

"Many waters cannot quench love; rivers cannot sweep it away."
Song of Songs 8:7a, NIV

Fire of My Love

"The fire of My love cannot be quenched with water. It is lit by the oil of My Spirit. The fire of My love is meant to consume and to change everything it touches. You are never the same when you encounter My love. Others are not the same when they encounter you, because you carry the fire of My love. Impact those around you. Change the atmosphere. Let My love ring out, loud and clear."

"But you are a chosen people, a royal priesthood,
a holy nation, God's special possession, that you
may declare the praises of him who called you
out of darkness into his wonderful light."
1 Peter 2:9, NIV

Treasure of My Presence

"The potential that lies within is worth drawing out. Others need what I have deposited within you. You need to realize the treasure that you carry. You are worthy. You are worth it. Choose to see you as I see you. Choose to see others as I see them. I have given you My perspective. Use it to propel you forth into the plans and purposes I have prepared for you. Go forth. Grow forth and be amazed at the results I will show you."

*"For we are God's handiwork, created in Christ
Jesus to do good works, which God prepared
in advance for us to do."*
Ephesians 2:10, NIV

Masterpiece Restored

"I am the repairer of the breach, the restorer of streets to dwell in. I have taken your rubble and removed it. Your slate is clean in Me. I am your firm foundation. I am the solid rock you can build on in confidence. Do not think that success is not for you. Do not think you lack the knowledge and skills to do what I have called you. I am the redeemer of the time you give Me. Trust Me to complete the work I began in you. You are My masterpiece. You are My work of art. I am with you in the finish; I am with you in the start."

"He replied, "If you have faith as small as a
mustard seed, you can say to this mulberry tree,
'Be uprooted and planted in the sea,'
and it will obey you."
Luke 17:6, NIV

Greatness in the Small

"I have given you what you need for increase. Do not despise the small. Much greatness lies within a small seed. Bring your best to Me and allow Me to cultivate a harvest within you. The tilling of the soil is your part. The increase is My part. We are partners forever. We are connected for life. Your success is My success. I have chosen to invest in you. See the potential you carry and take the courage to follow through. I see your best and I call it forth. The deep in Me calls to the deep in you."

"We love because he first loved us."
1 John 4:19, NIV

Choose Love

"I have given you a life to live more abundantly. Seek Me for wisdom in how to get the most out of the life I have given. I long to speak with you; you bring Me much joy and pleasure. When you turn aside from your busyness and turn, instead, toward Me, I am beyond delighted. You choose to spend time with Me. You choose to engage in the covenant we have made together! Love is a choice and you have chosen wisely whenever you choose to love Me. I have already chosen to love you! You are Mine and I am yours. Let this truth transform your soul."

"I will instruct you and teach you in the way you should go; I will counsel you with my loving eye on you."

Psalm 32:8, NIV

Guided by Love

"Apart from Me there is no other. No one loves you and designs your destiny like I do. We are meant to partner together; you and I, forever and ever. Look to Me and see your reflection in My eyes. I guide you with My eye upon you. You are never out of My sight. You are My desire. You are My design. You were not meant to hide. You are meant to shine. My glory is yours and your glory is Mine. Live in the rhythm of love divine."

*"But in your hearts revere Christ as Lord. Always
be prepared to give an answer to everyone who
asks you to give the reason for the hope that you
have. But do this with gentleness and respect,"*
1 Peter 3:15, NIV

Answer of Hope

"I have called you by name and you are Mine. I have called
you to let your light shine. The world in darkness is desperate
for hope. You have the answer hidden within. It is not meant
to stay within, but to be shared throughout. I have planted
My Spirit to grow forth with a shout; a shout that shatters the
deepest of fears. A shout that takes back what was stolen over
the years. You are the one I have chosen. You are the one I have
crowned. You are the one called to reverberate My sound."

"And the glory of the Lord will be revealed,
and all people will see it together. For the mouth
of the Lord has spoken."
Isaiah 40:5, NIV

Glory Revealed

"I have called you to Myself. I have called you to My own.
I have revealed to you the light that is to be shown. I have
placed within you the words to speak. I will draw those to you
that need to hear those words spoken. You will receive more
opportunities to reveal My glory. I am not finished with your
story. There is work to be done that only you can do. Your
obedience allows others to follow through. You carry more
influence than you can imagine. I am the one who goes before
and opens the door. Follow Me. Follow where I lead and trust
that I am leading you to a place that is best. Arise and take
hold of what I have for you. It has been on the shelf too long.
I restore you to your youth. You are as strong as before, if not
more so. Follow where I lead and take courage to go."

"...so is my word that goes out from my mouth:
It will not return to me empty, but will
accomplish what I desire and achieve
the purpose for which I sent it."
Isaiah 55:11, NIV

Word of Growth

"I have given you what you need. Do not despise the seed. Instead, sow it into the fertile soil of a faith filled heart and watch it grow! You will begin to see you and others as I see you. See and speak the good you see. Speak it forth and watch it grow. That which you focus on grows. Focus on Me and how I am at work in your life. You are not alone, not even in the midst of strife. I have given you power and strategies to be the one who rises to the top. I have called you to go. I will show you those things you must stop; behaviors and beliefs that no longer serve. Give them to Me and I will give you better behaviors and beliefs. I am in the business of transformation and I start with you."

"The voice of the Lord is powerful; the voice of the Lord is majestic."
Psalm 29:4, NIV

Power within My Name

"Your freedom will reign in the glory of My presence. You will feel the atmosphere shift at the mention of My name. Your love for Me is never in vain. I have come to set you free, so you can help to set others free. Your freedom is bigger than you. It expands beyond just you and encompasses those who will encounter you who need a touch from Me. Just one touch can set transformation on fire. When you see through My eyes, your circumstances are not as dire. Because you know that I am love and I sit above the circumstances. My love, and your position in Me, win the day always. You are more than a conqueror because you fight alongside Me. My glory in you is the light others see."

"Against all hope, Abraham in hope believed and so became the father of many nations, just as it had been said to him, "So shall your offspring be."
Romans 4:18, NIV

The Choice to Hope

"I have given you Me so you can be free. Enjoy the journey and revel in the delight of My love. I have your back. You need not fear lack. You have enough because I am more than enough. Trust Me with even your unspoken requests. That for which you are afraid to hope, choose to believe again. Dust off the doubt and dare to dream."

The King's Riches ©2017

"What you decide on will be done, and light will
shine on your ways."
Job 22:28, NIV

Speak the Truth that Transforms

"I am faithful to transform. Trust the hand of the One who designed you. I have a purpose and a plan you cannot see yet. But that does not mean it won't happen. As you yield to Me and believe in the truth you speak, it shall be established. It shall be done by My hand and your yielded mind and heart. How I delight the times when we are working together, not apart. I delight to do My will. I delight in you and you in Me. I have given you words to speak and eyes to see."

"Neither do people light a lamp and put it under a bowl. Instead they put it on its stand, and it gives light to everyone in the house."
Matthew 5:15, NIV

Be a Light

"Invest in others as I invest in you. There is much others can learn from you and much you can learn from others. You were not meant to hide. I have gifted you on purpose and for a purpose. If you do not share, and allow yourself to receive from others, you and they miss out on the potential that could be realized. Humility is the key that unlocks potential. The possibility of growth is exponential."

*"And without faith it is impossible to please God,
because anyone who comes to him must believe
that he exists and that he rewards those
who earnestly seek him."*
Hebrews 11:6, NIV

Rewards of Diligence

"I have declared that you are worthy. Believe this for yourself and you shall go far. To receive My reward, you must first believe that I am. I am the One whom you diligently seek. I am the One you will find. I will strengthen the weak. I am the One who can bind wounds with My word. I am faithful to speak that which I have heard. I declare the truth that I know and I watch the seed I have sown. I rejoice when I see it grow. It is the truth that you know that sets you free. The truth applied grows the tree. Your growth gives shelter and protection to others. Your growth is not just about you. This is why growth in Me is vital. There is a purpose to your growth, and a plan designed by Me. Seek and you will find. Knock and it will be open. I am the solid rock you can build your hope in."

*"So you are no longer a slave, but God's child;
and since you are his child, God has
made you also an heir."*
Galatians 4:7, NIV

Secrets Revealed

"Behold I have given you power and authority. You carry the seal of the King. It is embedded in the ring I have placed upon your hand when we became one in covenant with each other. I have claimed you as My own. Not as a slave, but as a son. A son knows what his father is doing. A father cares to share with his son. Listen and respond to what I will tell you. It is to your great benefit to listen and obey. Listen, learn and reap the rewards. I will never steer you wrong. My power is within you. When you speak forth My words you bring that power to the surface that it may do what it is designed to do. Transformation transpires and inspires others."

"The boundary lines have fallen for me in
pleasant places; surely I have a
delightful inheritance."
Psalm 16:6, NIV

Lines of Inheritance

"Come take My hand and follow Me. I have much to show you. You will see the closer we become, that your security is found in Me. Not a box or shell of limitations. No, I am a God of limitless love and I am the one who declares the lines of your land. You need not fear when you are with Me. My plans for you are good! My desire for you is freedom from that which has held you back. You were designed to journey with Me. Not only do I go to the low places, but I venture to the high places too. The view is much more glorious when shared with you. I delight to see the joy on your face. I love to hear the lilt in your laughter. I desire only the best for My best. Oh that you would believe Me and the love I so desire to give you when you are open to receive. Take My hand and follow Me. I have much to show you."

*"Then your light will break forth like the dawn,
and your healing will quickly appear; then your
righteousness will go before you, and the glory
of the Lord will be your rear guard."*
Isaiah 58:8, NIV

I Am Your Rear Guard

"I am your comfort zone. Comfort is found in Me. When you know that I go before you, with you and after you, you will find the security you feel you lack. You will be confident that I have your back. Trust Me to lead you. Trust yourself to follow. The foundation you stand on is firm, not hollow. I have widened your path and established your steps. Go where I go and speak what I say. Go make an impact on others this day. I have people in mind for you to bless and encourage. Stay open to Me and those I will reveal. Speak the words I say. A word fitly spoken has the power to heal."

"As water reflects the face, so one's life
reflects the heart."
Proverbs 27:19, NIV

True Reflection

"I am your rhyme and you are My reason. I am the words and you are My melody. The song I sing over you is a song of love. I desire to spend time with you. Do you feel the same? I am your strong and mighty tower. I am your shelter from the rain. I speak to you words of life, love and hope. Open the eyes of your heart and the ears of your mind so you can see and hear what I am speaking to you. I have not left you and I never will. I have designed for you a purpose that only you can fill. No one is exactly like you. You are unique and original and lovely. See the beauty I see in you this day. Let Me be your mirror; your true reflection."

"Therefore I tell you, whatever you ask for in prayer, believe that you have received it, and it will be yours."
Mark 11:24, NIV

Ask for the Answer

"I have given you solutions to problems. If you do not know, ask Me and I will tell you. Believe that I answer. Believe that I hear. When you take courage and ask, My heart is filled with cheer. I have given you Me for such a time as this. I have given you skills and tactics to use. The outcome is up to Me. However, you must choose. Choose to bless others with what I have blessed you with. My love is real. It is no myth."

*"I will make you into a great nation, and I will
bless you; I will make your name great, and you
will be a blessing. I will bless those who bless
you, and whoever curses you I will curse; and all
peoples on earth will be blessed through you."*
Genesis 12:2-3, NIV

Seeds Sown Multiply

"I have given you all you need for life and godliness. Use what I
have given you and watch it multiply. I desire you to succeed,
more than you want to succeed. Know that I am for you, not
against you. You and Me are on the same team, and we both
win. I have given you a victor's spirit; a drive and determination
to win and to right wrongs. I am the God of justice and I
prevail. No longer will you cower in fear. I am the God courage
and I am here. You will know I go before. You will know that I
am yours forevermore."

"For we are God's handiwork, created in Christ
Jesus to do good works, which God prepared
in advance for us to do."
Ephesians 2:10, NIV

A Work of Wonder

"I have declared My wonders to perform. You will see Me move mightily on your behalf. Not only so you know that I am He, but so others may also see Me. I am the One who is forever. I am the One who is concerned about what concerns you. Yes, I crafted the world, but My best work was you! Go forth in the confidence that you do not go alone. You go armed with Me. I go before you, with you and after you. I am the One who fights for you. You are the one in whom I delight. You bring Me much pleasure. Oh that you would believe this truth. What a force we can be, when you know your true identity."

The King's Riches ©2017

"The purposes of a person's heart are deep waters,
but one who has insight draws them out."
Proverbs 20:5, NIV

Desire to Greatness

"I have given you My desires. My desires are your desires
because we share the same heart, you and I. I reveal Myself
to you time and again, because you have been proven
trustworthy to share with. Greatness lies within you, and I
come alongside you to help draw it out. Others need what I
have given you. Give and you shall receive more. My love and
truth are an endless supply. Ask for the more I have waiting
for you. Increase your capacity, your mindset for more. Let Me
overwhelm you with My love and goodness. It is yours in Me. It
is for today and tomorrow. There is plenty! Trust Me to supply
you with all you need and then some. It is the protocol of the
kingdom you have inherited and inhabited."

"For he has rescued us from the dominion of darkness and brought us into the kingdom of the Son he loves,"
Colossians 1:13, NIV

Transformation

"It is in the heat of the moment that causes transformation. The striking of the heated metal causes it to be shaped for the purpose of its intention. So, too, the heat created between you and I will cause your heart and life to expand. You must possess this land. The land I have gifted you with must be enjoyed by you. It is for you. I have drawn the lines of your land in pleasant places and I call you to inhabit. Just as I have inhabited your heart. You have set aside a place for Me to dwell deep in the midst of you. Rest well in the knowledge that you are not alone because with you, your heart is My home. Praise and gratitude are the keys that keep your heart open to Me. Watch and see what I will do on behalf of the one who is open! I am the solid rock that you can place your hope in."

"My sheep listen to my voice; I know them,
and they follow me."
John 10:27, NIV

Hope to Hear My Voice

"Do not doubt this hope I placed inside you. You are meant to shine, not hide. I have given you words to speak that others need to hear. Sometimes I shout, sometimes I cheer, but always I am speaking to you. You are My own and I love to interact with you one on one. I am not too busy and you are not too unimportant. Believe in the value and worth I have placed in you and others. See you and others through the lens of My love. Enlarge your vision and expand your reach. I repair many a breach. I am the One who fills in the gaps. I bind up wounds and give tools to use in attacks. We fight as one to reinforce the victory won."

"They will be like a tree planted by the water that sends out its roots by the stream. It does not fear when heat comes; its leaves are always green. It has no worries in a year of drought and never fails to bear fruit."
Jeremiah 17:8, NIV

Prepare to be Fruitful

"I have given you a desire to know Me more. I give you My riches in exchange for your poor. You were not designed to lack. You were designed to be fruitful. A fruitful tree nourishes everyone who will decide to take and eat. Notice they must first take and then eat. Action is a crucial step in fruition. To ready the soil to receive the seed, the ground must be tilled. Do not be afraid to prepare. Preparation propels one into their desired result. I have many desired results for you. Prepare your heart in Me. Speak My words that will set others free."

"The Lord said, "If as one people speaking the
same language they have begun to do this, then
nothing they plan to do will be
impossible for them."
Genesis 11:6, NIV

Aligned for Influence

"I have called you to invest in others. See their worth through
My eyes and call forth the potential they cannot yet see in
them. Others need you and you need others. I will show you,
if you ask who you are to be aligned with. Who are you to
influence and be influenced by? The right connections make all
the difference in the world. I have connected Myself to you and
because you have chosen to be connected to Me, your world
has changed. Your life has changed because of your decisions.
This is why we must choose wisely. The wise decisions can
skyrocket you and others on the trajectory of destiny."

"Jesus looked at them and said, "With man this is impossible, but with God all things are possible."
Matthew 19:26, NIV

Believe for the Possible

"I have given you My spirit of wisdom and discernment. You do not walk alone. I have set My Spirit within you to be your helper, guide and comfort. Ask when you need help. You are not weak for the asking. Asking opens the door of communication because it encourages conversation between you and I. This is how it should be. This is what I desire: to have a living, breathing, walking, talking relationship with the best of My creation. You are My best. You are My favorite. You are My original. No other will do. You must see you through the eyes of Me, if you are to walk forward in victory. Believe it is possible, because it is!"

The King's Riches ©2017

"The boundary lines have fallen for me in pleasant places; surely I have a delightful inheritance."
Psalm 16:6, NIV

The Portion in My Presence

"I have given you portions to tend and to keep. I have given you land that did not come cheap. The gifts I give are costly, but they are also meant to be enjoyed. Enjoy this day laid out before you. Enjoy the people I place on your path. Be carriers of My presence, laborers of My light. I will take the wrongs and make them right. I am the repairer of the breach and I give you a firm foundation. Build upon the truth of Me."

"You are the light of the world. A town built on a hill cannot be hidden. Neither do people light a lamp and put it under a bowl. Instead they put it on its stand, and it gives light to everyone in the house. In the same way, let your light shine before others, that they may see your good deeds and glorify your Father in heaven."
Matthew 5:14-16, NIV

City of Hope and Light

"I have given you My joy to share with others. Take time to look around and see who needs what I have given you. You are My delight and I am delighted when you share with others. Darkness cannot hide in a room filled with light. You are My city on a hill, meant to shine. I have placed My hope within so others can be partakers of love divine. Who can you bless today? Whose burden can you lighten? Do not fear rejection of man. Lean on and follow Me. I am the One with the plan."

*"For I know the plans I have for you," declares the
Lord, "plans to prosper you and not to harm you,
plans to give you hope and a future."*
Jeremiah 29:11, NIV

Planned on Purpose

"You exist on purpose and for a purpose. This purpose is far
beyond what you can think or imagine. I have set eternity in
your heart, so you can have an eternal impact. Reach beyond
that which you know, and take courage to change and grow.
I transform you from glory to glory for My glory. All I do is
because of you and My desire for you to know Me. When you
choose to know and be known by Me, your transparency will
breed the freedom you seek. You are armed with strength and
fit for My purposes. I have built within you a desire to please
Me. Not because you must earn My love, but because My love is
free for the enjoying. Rest in My love; let My glory shine within
you. Bring the truth to others so they, too, can be transformed."

*"The Lord bless you and keep you; the Lord make
his face shine on you and be gracious to you;
the Lord turn his face toward you and
give you peace."*
Numbers 6:24-26, NIV

Face Shining with Glory

"I have made a way for you. I have made room for your gifts to be used and displayed in My glory. I have written your story with care and purpose and delight. I have called you forth from dark to light. My love has smoothed out your wrinkles of worry, and My grace has made your complexion glorious. Mine is the love reflected in your eyes. Show others My love. Let them see Me in you. You are a conduit of transformation. You are a carrier of My presence. You are a joy and a delight to know. You have much to offer. Ask Me and I will show you your true value and worth. You are the smile on My face and the lilt in My laughter. I am yours now and forever after."

The King's Riches ©2017

"He has filled them with skill to do all kinds of
work as engravers, designers, embroiderers in
blue, purple and scarlet yarn and fine linen,
and weavers—all of them skilled
workers and designers."
Exodus 35:35, NIV

Improving Gifts of Skill

"I have what you have need of in order to advance . You will not see these tools in their finished form. It will become clearer the more you use them. Talent develops the more you use it. Step out in faith and watch the growth that will happen before you. I have your back. You can trust there is nothing you will lack. I have come alongside to take your arm and lead you. I have placed others on your path to help you along as well. You need them as much as they need you. Ask Me to show you who. Who have I aligned you with to exceed and excel your strengths? I make room for you. There is plenty of space to practice your gift."

"The voice of the Lord is over the waters;
the God of glory thunders, the Lord thunders
over the mighty waters. The voice of the Lord is
powerful; the voice of the Lord is majestic."
Psalm 29:3-4, NIV

Power of the Word

"I have given you all things pertaining to life and godliness. You have what you need to begin stepping out into all I have for you. I want the best for you. I am faithful and true. That which I begin, I will complete. I will not leave you. I will not abandon My work unfinished. I am the God of the complete. I finish what I start and I do what I say. I am with you in the night and day. Share what I speak to you. My word spoken forth gives you much advantage into what I have planned for you. Partner with Me and we will see things and go places you could only have imagined. I am calling you to dream again. See as possible what you could not even imagine probable. I am He who created your imagination. Use it for My glory. Have faith and take courage. Choose to write your own story. You can do it. I believe in you!"

"The Lord has done it this very day; let us
rejoice today and be glad."
Psalm 118:24, NIV

Day of Rejoicing

"I have called this a day for rejoicing. As you make it a habit to reflect on Me and My ways, you will find ever-increasing joy. You will see that I am your advocate. You will see My presence in your present. You will know that I am for you, not against you. You are the one who brings joy to My heart. I am the one who will never part. I am with you in the valley and I am with you on the mountain. You will see and know that you are not alone. I have made a plan and I desire you to know Me more. You will see Me in your everyday as you grow more sensitive to My presence. I am here. I am near. I hear you even when you whisper. When you do not know what to say, ask Me and I will help you pray. You do not have to know all the answers. That is My job. Your job is to trust Me and obey. Follow where I am leading. You will know the joy that seems fleeting. In My presence is peace and fullness of joy."

"Elisha replied to her, "How can I help you? Tell me, what do you have in your house?""Your servant has nothing there at all," she said, "except a small jar of olive oil." Elisha said, "Go around and ask all your neighbors for empty jars. Don't ask for just a few. Then go inside and shut the door behind you and your sons. Pour oil into all the jars, and as each is filled, put it to one side."
2 Kings 4:2-4, NIV

Provision has been Provided

"You already have more than you need to begin. Follow My lead, step out in faith, and watch how I work in your life. I am with you every step of the way. My presence will guide you to where you have never been before. You were not meant to sidle in fear. You are meant to soar with confidence. I have given you direction and I love to see your fears fall as your faith takes flight. In moments of doubt and uncertainty, look to the constant one: Me. As you follow in faith, you lead the charge for others to follow suit. I have prepared you for more than you are currently experiencing. This truly is a time of rejoicing. Dance to the rhythm of the beat of My heart. It has been Me from the start."

"You are the light of the world. A town built on a hill cannot be hidden."
Matthew 5:14, NIV

A Light Meant to Shine Bright

"I have created your map. I am your guide. Come into the light. You are not meant to hide. People are looking at Me in you. It is not about your inadequacies. It is about your obedience. What can I do with a heart that is humble toward Me? You are the one I have called worthy and clean. I know what I am doing, even if you do not. I am in charge of the details. Trust Me to get you to where you need to go. I have gone before you and have prepared the way. I have ordered your footsteps. Will you align your day to My design? I lead, but you choose to follow. Each action is a choice you must first choose to take. I will show you the way to go. It is My desire for you to know Me more. The table is set and the feast is ready. Enter into the best I have for you."

"When he ascended on high, he took many captives and gave gifts to his people."
Ephesians 4:8, NIV

Gifts Given and Received

"I have aligned you with those who are beneficial for you. You will know them by their love, their willingness to encourage and share what I have given them. Know this: they have need of you as well. You have much to offer. There is an ebb and flow of giving and receiving. This is the course of relationship that I have outlined from the beginning. Just as I need you and you need Me, so others need you and you need them. I am calling you forth to engage the gifts that have been dormant for far too long. Gifts that have gone unnoticed by even you because you have not claimed them as gifts. What have I given to you that you enjoy? Start and share there. It is not as difficult as it seems. Recognize, acknowledge, and plant the seed. Get ready for the harvest. It will surely come. Planting is not the end of the process. For every planting, there comes a reaping. Engage in the process and keep on believing."

"I no longer call you servants, because a servant
does not know his master's business. Instead,
I have called you friends, for everything that I
learned from my Father I have made
known to you."
John 15:15, NIV

Friend of the King

"I have shown you the wonders of Me, time and time again. I am the one who calls you friend. I am the one who has chosen to spend time with you. Will you let Me do what I do? I will show you different facets of Me if you will be still and listen to what I will share with you. You will see Me at work in your life in ever-increasing ways. I delight in your delight of Me. I delight in seeing you free. I have made a spectacle of your enemies. You will know the triumph of victory. I have called you to win and win and win again. To the victor go the spoils and I am content in spoiling you to the fullest. I lavish My love upon you. I do so with joy. You are not a burden. You are a blessing. You are not in the way. You are right where you need to be; next to Me and listening to what I say. You are My dream come true. You are the reflection you see in My eyes. I love to love and I love to surprise!"

*"But from everlasting to everlasting the Lord's
love is with those who fear him, and his
righteousness with their children's children."*
Psalm 103:17, NIV

Everlasting Love

"I am from everlasting to everlasting. I have always been and always will be. I am always been on the scene, even when it is difficult to see. Ask Me to show you My glory. I will reveal to you what you have already known but were afraid to grasp. The table has been set, the provision has been provided. It is found in Me. I am the one who guards and guides. I lead you forth into the best I have for you. I have already prepared for you. I am the way. Do not fear. There is no lack in the abundance of Me. You have been given you the tools and resources to succeed. I invest in you because I know your true value. I see your true you and I call it forth. Embrace your value. Enjoy the journey. There is much to learn in the playing out of our story. I invite you in to rest in My presence. My peace is evident. My joy overflows."

"And we all, who with unveiled faces contemplate the Lord's glory, are being transformed into his image with ever-increasing glory, which comes from the Lord, who is the Spirit."
2 Corinthians 3:18, NIV

From Glory to Glory

"You are My indispensible one. You cannot be duplicated or replaced. There is only one like you for a reason. So you may know that I love you uniquely. Ask Me what I love about you. I am longing you to ask. I gives Me great joy to answer you. Ask Me how I see you and be ready to hear and receive the truth of My love. My love transforms. I have loved watching you become the beauty that you are. My glory transforms you from the inside out. I am not done creating. I am still doing a work in and through you. You have My attention always. You are forever on My mind and in My heart. Together we are one. Together we reveal the glory of Me. As you trust the process and rest in My love, you will both see and reflect My beauty."

"The Lord himself goes before you and will be with you; he will never leave you nor forsake you. Do not be afraid; do not be discouraged."
Deuteronomy 31:8, NIV

His Ever-constant Presence

"I have gifted you with the present. I have gifted you with My presence. I go before you, with you and after you. My hand is upon you and I guide you with My eye. Look to Me to see where I am leading. I will give you wisdom and understanding liberally if you ask. If you were not capable, I would not call you to the task. I believe in you for so much more. Follow Me through the open door. The time has come and the table is set. Take your place and rejoice. You are not forgotten. Not even for a day. I have always been here, and will always stay. Enter in and receive what I have set aside for you."

"For the Lord takes delight in his people; he
crowns the humble with victory."
Psalm 149:4, NIV

Delighting in You

"It is My good pleasure to delight your heart. I have loved you from the start. I am altogether lovely and so are you. I have given you what you need and more. My love is an open door. I have given you access to Me at any time. I desire to speak with you. I know what you are going to say, but I want to hear you tell it. I love to hear your voice. Time spent with Me is your choice. Oh how I delight in our times together. You do not have to need anything dire to sit with Me. I am never too busy for you. If you do not know what to say, just sit and listen to what I have to say. It is not about having the right words. I will give you the words when you need them. I am speaking to you each day. Life will happen when you take time to listen. Never forget I am right here waiting for you. My door is always open. I am the one you can hang your hope on."

"He has made everything beautiful in its time. He has also set eternity in the human heart; yet no one can fathom what God has done from beginning to end."
Ecclesiastes 3:11, NIV

Fullness of Time

"I desire you to come closer. There is no need to fear My love. It is for you, just as I have said. I do not say things to not do them. What I have promised will come to pass. Trust Me for the timing of the fulfillment of it all. Trust that I know the end from the beginning. The results are marvelous. You will be amazed. You were born to be amazing, to show up ready to show you. You are meant to be revealed, not hidden. A lamp hidden under a basket does not light a room. I have called you to light up a room, to light up the lives I have connected you with. You have need of others just as they have need of you. You all hold inherent value and worth. See you and others through the lens of Me. I will align your sight and establish your steps. You grow stronger as you are aligned with Me. We are a force of love to be reckoned with."

*"Arise, shine, for your light has come, and the
glory of the Lord rises upon you."*
Isaiah 60:1, NIV

Time for Awakening

"I am awakening your heart to love. I am awakening your heart to Me. The love you have seen Me bestow on others is for you, as well. You are not excluded. You are very much included. There is a place at the table just for you. If you do not take your place your seat sits empty. No one else can fill the position I have given you. No one else can gift the world with the unique gifts I have given you. Know that you are that cherished. You are that planned for. You are loved so deeply and so much more. Choose to sit at the table of relationship with Me. I have blessed you with more than you need to begin. Start where you are and follow the steps I lead you in."

*"Against all hope, Abraham in hope believed and
so became the father of many nations, just as it
had been said to him, "So shall your
offspring be."*
Romans 418, NIV

Days of Hope

"Gone are the days of doubt and worry. I am on the scene and I bring hope and assurance. Ask Me to show you your supply. I will show you and give you strategies to receive that which is yours. Believe what I reveal is for you. I am causing you to see the provision that has been there just beneath the surface. I give you tools to unearth the treasure within. Take the first step and begin. I have called you to adventure. I have called you to My side. You are called to be seen, not to hide. I will reveal Myself to you in ways that amaze. Get ready to receive, rejoice and believe."

"The Lord replied, "My Presence will go with you,
and I will give you rest."
Exodus 33:14, NIV

Peace of My Presence

"I am making you aware of My presence. I am with you at every turn. I am speaking to you in ways that you would not expect. I am a creative God and the language of My love has many dialects. Be open to receive. Be open to hearing Me answer you in astounding ways. I am intimately involved in even the smallest details. You will recognize Me by the peace of My Spirit that resides inside. I have given you the very nature of Me. You are never alone. I look at you as one who loves beyond measure. One who wants the absolute best for His treasure. Be ready to hear the words I speak. I will answer those who seek."

"For with you is the fountain of life; in your light we see light."
Psalm 36:9, NIV

I Delight in Your Love

"You have captured My heart with one glance of your eyes. I am the one who loves to surprise. I surprise you with My love when you least expect it. The joy on your face makes surprising you more than worth it. Watch Me work on your behalf. Know that I am on the move. I am opening your eyes so you can see the doors of opportunities I have opened for you. You will see those who are to be on your team. You are not meant to go it alone. Together we go forth to explore the land laid out for you. It is for you. I have given you the best of Me. Will you trust Me with the rest of you? It takes courage to trust that I have your back, that I have your best interests at heart. I will give you the courage you need, if you ask. You are strong and worthy and up for the task. Follow My lead. Take the seed I have given and sow where I show. You will see the wonders of Me grow."

"I will instruct you and teach you in the way you
should go; I will counsel you with my
loving eye on you."
Psalm 32:8, NIV

Direction

"I am the treasure you receive when you stop letting fear get in the way. The light within you is Me and I am shining brighter each day. Each day you say yes to My plans and purposes for you, is a day that you move forward into the best of Me. I am giving you the direction you seek. I am giving you the wisdom you have asked for. I am your Deliverer and so much more. You are My delight and it is My good pleasure to serve you well. When you choose that which serves you best over that which serves you the least, it will cause you to rise. You are My anointed one and your gifts have been supplied. Why are you looking for the dominate gift? All are important and all have great benefits as they are released. I am the treasure you carry. My word will come to pass. The time approaches, the time is here."

"I am the gate; whoever enters through me will be saved. They will come in and go out, and find pasture."
John 10:9, NIV

Open Door to More

"I am the one who created you for more. I am the way. I am the door. I have given you access to Me and the abundant life I have provided. I will lead you if you choose to be guided. I lead you in the way everlasting. You will know this hope that I offer. Engage with Me and the gifts that I give. Seek Me and find Me. Have faith and live. Live the life I have designed exclusively for you. I am a personal Jesus who is revealing Myself to you in very real and personal ways. I am revealing My truth to you in ways that will resonate. I have called you to love, not hate. You will know the joy that I give. Resting in Me gives you the strength to go forth in boldness. You are My mouthpiece and I have given you much to say. Speak My words of truth this day."

*"The Lord replied, "My Presence will go with
you, and I will give you rest."*
Exodus 33:14, NIV

Gift of My Presence

"I have gifted you with the gift of My presence. I am with you
always. Ask Me where I am at work in your life. I will show you
that I am on the scene. Even when I am working behind the
scenes, rest assured, I am at work in your life for you highest
good. I am the one who leads you in the way I have laid out
for you. I am calling you deeper into Me. In following Me into
the depths, you will know greater dimensions of My love. You
will experience the peace unshakable. You will know the joy
unspeakable. I am the one who crafted the details. I am inviting
you on the journey. Even when you do not know all the details
beforehand, trust Me that I know what you do not. I will get us
there. Hope and do not doubt. I am the Breaker who has gone
up with a shout."

"...but let the one who boasts boast about this:
that they have the understanding to know me,
that I am the Lord, who exercises kindness,
justice and righteousness on earth, for in
these I delight, declares the Lord."
Jeremiah 9:24, NIV

Glory of Being Known

"Know that I know you. I am your Creator and I know you inside and out. I know you better than you know yourself. I see you and I hear you, more often than you think. There is nowhere you go that I am not there. I collect your tears and count your hair. Invite Me into the whole of your day. I will show you where I am present in your present. You will know that you are not alone. I have made you My forever home. I have filled you with joy unspeakable and full of glory. Ask Me to reveal to you more of your story. Gather your courage and join Me on the journey. There are many wonders all around. I am awakening your ears to hear the sound. You are found by Me and set apart for My glory. Your yielding to Me gets you ready for the more I have for you. Remember I am Faithful. Remember I am true."

"Where there is no revelation, people cast off restraint; but blessed is the one who heeds wisdom's instruction."
Proverbs 29:18, NIV

Vision for Provision

"Have no fear. The answer is here. Before you called, I answered. I am revealing to you where I am at work in your life. Rest assured, I am on the scene. I am work for your highest good. I want more for you than you can even hope to imagine. I am expanding your sphere of influence and enhancing your field of vision. You will see Me at work in the smallest and largest details. I am aligning your vision and tuning your heart to the frequency of Me. You will hear Me more and more clearly the more we spend time with one another. Time spent with Me is multiplied not divided. I am the accelerator of that which you have been waiting for. Get ready. Dare to dream. Dare to hope. Dare to ask. I am longing to show Myself strong on your behalf. Ask that you may receive. Open your heart and mind to believe."

"Now the Lord is the Spirit, and where the Spirit
of the Lord is, there is freedom."
2 Corinthians 3:17, NIV

Spirit-led Liberty

"I have come to give you life abundantly. I am opening your eyes so you can see. I am opening your ears so you can hear. Peace, be still. Know I am drawing you near. I am calling you forth to more of Me. I am drawing your heart into the best I have for you. You bring such joy to My heart I can hardly stand it. The beauty in you shines brighter than you have been able to see. I am calling you to be the best you that you can be. My Spirit inside sets your heart and mind to liberty. You are free to explore the more. Free to inhabit the land of inheritance. It is yours for the receiving; yours for the enjoying. I have placed My best in you to set you forth. I am calling you into adventure with Me. Look at Me and get ready to sail the high sees."

"Lift up your eyes and look to the heavens: Who created all these? He who brings out the starry host one by one and calls forth each of them by name. Because of his great power and mighty strength, not one of them is missing."
Isaiah 40:26, NIV

Seek and See

"I have gifted you with the ability to see as I see. It is a skill honed by spending time with Me. In My presence you will gain My perspective. Ask Me to show you what I have for you. Ask Me to reveal how I am at work on your behalf. I will reassure you that I have been here all along. I have your best interests at heart. I lead you along the path called straight as you pray from a place called done. It is finished. The task is complete. The battle has been won. No need for despair or defeat. I call you to come boldly to the throne of Me. Speak what you want. Do not let fear have its way. As you speak forth your deepest concerns and desires, you will see that I am more than able to answer. Trust Me for what you have not dared to ask. Ask big. I am up for the task."

*"Enter his gates with thanksgiving and his courts
with praise; give thanks to him and
praise his name."*
Psalm 100:4, NIV

Thanksgiving for the Harvest

"I have planted the seed in you. Till the ground with thanksgiving. Rejoice in the harvest on the horizon. I have given you the courage to ask for you want. Know that I have your best interests at heart. What I have for others, I have for you, too. You are not the exception, you are exceptional. You are My excellent one created to do mighty exploits. I have set your heart on a journey of discovery. I have skilled you that you may be a blessing wherever you go. I will show you what to say and to whom. I am opening doors of opportunity and influence. Others have need of what I have given you. Share freely. Love deeply. Know that I am the one at work behind the scenes and center stage in your transformation. Yield to Me with childlike faith and honesty."

"Before they call I will answer; while they are
still speaking I will hear."
Isaiah 65:24, NIV

Call Answered

"I have seen your heart tender towards Me. You have not gone unnoticed. Your prayers will not go unanswered. I have heard your cries and I will answer. Before you call I answer and while you are still speaking, I hear. Get ready to receive that which you have longed for. I have placed it in your heart and on your mind for a purpose. Why so downcast? Hope in Me. Know I care. I see. I hear. I answer. I am at work on your behalf. Ask Me to reveal My presence to you. I am right here. I am eager for you to see that you are not forgotten. I will watch over My word to perform it. I am He who is faithful and true. I am the giver of life and keeper of My word. I shine forth upon you as you lift your eyes and tune your ears to Me. Trust that I am for you. Wait and watch. See what I will do."

*"You have stolen my heart, my sister, my bride;
you have stolen my heart with one glance of
your eyes, with one jewel of your necklace."*
Song of Songs 4:9, NIV

One Glance Sets the Heart to Dance

"My plans for you are good, because I am good. I do not think evil of you. I love you more than you think I do. More than you think I have a right to. I decide how much I love you. It is not based on your performance or lack thereof. It has been decided from the beginning that I love you lavishly. I love you uniquely. I reveal My love to you in ways that are deeply personal and undoubtedly true. It is My good pleasure to delight in you. I delight in the way your smile lights up a room. You have power to shift the atmosphere of where you are, just by showing up and being you. Be who I have designed you to be; to be anything less is robbing others of joy of knowing and loving you as you are. Make no excuses or apologies. Let My love transform and reform your thinking and your seeing. I am on the scene and I am causing you to see what you have not yet seen. Allow Me to do My work in you. There is much to be done and it requires your best you to shine through."

*"Arise, shine, for your light has come, and the
glory of the Lord rises upon you."*
Isaiah 60:1, NIV

Called to Shine

"I have seen you in the hidden places where no one else could
see. I am calling you forth into who I have designed you to be.
You do not belong hidden and afraid. You were made for more.
You were made to be brave. I have declared your end from the
beginning. Your mode of operation is winning, not losing. I
have set your feet on the path marked straight. I am there right
with you guiding you along. You will know I am here. I have
been here the entire time. We are one. I am yours and you are
Mine. Take courage. Take heart. I will make the way clear. You
sail with Me. Allow Me to steer. We will arrive to the desired
destination. Trust and believe I will take you there. I know what
you need. I collect every tear and I hear every prayer."

"Praise be to the Lord my Rock, who trains my
hands for war, my fingers for battle."
Psalm 144:1, NIV

Training for Reigning

"I have given you an answer. I have given you the solution you seek. You are growing in grace and love. You are strong, not weak. I have made you mighty on My behalf. I have given you skills to use. I have trained and am training you to wisely use the gifts I have given. You will grow in grace and favor with God and man. You will enter and inhabit your land. It is for you. My blessings are for you. You are not forgotten, as you sometimes suppose. Your garden is lovely, as it grows and grows. Take the steps forward I will show you. You need not fear. I am always here. You do not go alone. There is no reason to hide. I have called you to arise and shine. Others need to Me in you. You are the one I have chosen to do mighty exploits in Me. Embrace the assignment. Get ready for more. I am the way. I am the door."

"The Lord appeared to us in the past, saying:
I have loved you with an everlasting love; I have
drawn you with unfailing kindness."
Jeremiah 31:3, NIV

Everlasting Love

"I have loved you with an everlasting love; a love for all seasons that will not be denied. You will see Me at work in your life more and more. As we spend more time and learn more about each other, you will begin to see Me in everything you do. Day-to-day occurrences will reveal Me to you in ways you have not thought of before. It is the gift of My presence. It is the blessing of your faith. I honor you and your faithfulness to Me. You reveal your heart to Me each time you choose to believe. Each time you choose to trust Me with your concerns. You know that it is I who cares for you. As you settle in and make your home in Me, you will have a fresh perspective from which to see. The eyes of your faith will be enlightened. You will know your future has brightened. I am the one who calls you near. I am the one always here."

"Rejoice in the Lord always. I will say it again:
Rejoice!"
Philippians 4:4, NIV

Gratefulness

"When you receive that for which you have asked, do not be afraid to rejoice. I have seen. I have heard. I have answered. It does My heart so good to see you fully embracing My goodness. Such rejoicing reveals that you believe I am good and you are worthy to receive that which I have laid aside for you. Rejoice in the revealing of your inheritance. Your legacy will not be cut off. I have mighty plans for you. Great is My faithfulness. My greatness is unsearchable. Who can see and know all that I have for them? Trust is the key that unlocks the chains that have held you captive. You will see and know that you are free. You are free to enjoy Me and free to let Me enjoy you. You are My delight. You are secure in Me. There is no reason for fright."

"Call to me and I will answer you and tell you
great and unsearchable things you do not know."
Jeremiah 33:3, NIV

Call and I will Answer

"There has never been a moment when I have not seen you. You have never been hidden from Me. You have always been on My mind and in My heart. I am drawing you forth in love. Know that My heart is not hidden from you. I long to reveal Myself to you more and more. Not only so you can know you more, but also so you can know Me more. Know that I have never left you. I am right here. You always have access to Me. Just say the word and I will show you I am at work in even the smallest details of your life. I am here in the midst of both joy and strife. You have longed to be seen. Know that you have never been hidden. You have been protected, loved and cared for even before day one began. You have always been and will always be in My hand. Ask Me to show you. I will reveal. My love redeems. My love does heal."

*"She is more precious than rubies; nothing you
desire can compare with her."*
Proverbs 3:15, NIV

More Precious than Rubies

"You are My joy, My pearl of great price. You are worth more than diamonds and gold. You bring delight to My heart and a smile to My soul! You did not know what you were missing until I made your broken, whole. I am the repairer. I am the restorer. I polish you to restore you to your natural beauty. The table is set. The best china is used. You are worth celebrating. Do not refuse. You bring Me glory and honor when you allow your greatness to shine. The world will know that you are Mine."

*"Now the Lord is the Spirit, and where the Spirit
of the Lord is, there is freedom."*
2 Corinthians 3:17, NIV

My Spirit Brings Liberty

"When you move forward in freedom, others are allowed to move forward as well. Your freedom sets others freedom in motion. I am the catalyst that sets you on a specific course of action. Lean close to hear what I say. Take courage and obey. Blessings follow the one who obeys. I desire to bless you. You fill My heart with such joy. Oh that you would experience just a bit of the love I have for you, you would be forever changed. I love you as you are, and I want what is best for you. Rejoice that you hear My voice. Your obedience shall take you far and ignite the hope that I have placed within you. Blaze the trail of hope that will cause others to follow suit. You are My desire and I am in hot pursuit."

"Therefore, since we are surrounded by such
a great cloud of witnesses, let us throw off
everything that hinders and the sin that so easily
entangles. And let us run with perseverance
the race marked out for us,"
Hebrews 12:1, NIV

Lay Aside the Weight

"In the name of love, lay aside pride. Lay aside that which so easily entangles. The struggle is not worth the strife. I have died to give you a better life. Embrace the hope and joy I bring. Do not be afraid to laugh and sing. You are the delight of My heart and I desire you to feel and embrace the lightness and the weightiness of My love. Enjoy you. Enjoy others. Enjoy Me. Embrace the life that is yours for the taking. I will heal that which is broken. Declare My name. Declare the word I have spoken."

The King's Riches ©2017

*"In a large house there are articles not only of
gold and silver, but also of wood and clay; some
are for special purposes and some for common
use. 21 Those who cleanse themselves from the
latter will be instruments for special purposes,
made holy, useful to the Master and
prepared to do any good work."*
2 Timothy 2:20-21, NIV

You are My Vessel of Honor

"I have given you skills to practice. As you are faithful in
practicing, you will see Me faithful in increasing your skills. To
practice is to stay humble and teachable. A teachable heart is
a tender heart. I can pour into an open vessel. I and the world
have need of the skills I have given you. Do not let fear and
uncertainty keep you from My best. Trust Me and you will see
Me at work on your behalf. Be sensitive to My Spirit, and quick
to answer the call. I celebrate you when you rise, and I lift you
when you fall."

*"For we are God's handiwork, created in Christ
Jesus to do good works, which God prepared
in advance for us to do."*
Ephesians 2:10, NIV

My Workmanship Created for Good Works

"Hear Me speak to you your worth. Repeat My words back to you. You will know the truth that will set you free from your limiting mindsets. You are not meant to feel less than. I have designed you for success. That success is found in Me. It is found in us working together. Be who I have called you to be. You are My masterpiece designed to make a difference and to add value to all who encounter you."

*"Now to him who is able to do immeasurably
more than all we ask or imagine, according to
his power that is at work within us,"*
Ephesians 3:20 NIV

More than You Can Think or Imagine

"I am the One who leads you in the dance. Take courage and take a chance. I have your best in mind for you. I am He who is forever faithful and forever true. You belong to Me and I belong to you. Dare to achieve that for which you dared not hope. I have placed My desires within you. With joy you shall draw from the supply of Me. I am the One who rejoices that you are free."

"But if serving the Lord seems undesirable to you, then choose for yourselves this day whom you will serve, whether the gods your ancestors served beyond the Euphrates, or the gods of the Amorites, in whose land you are living. But as for me and my household, we will serve the Lord."
Joshua 24:15 NIV

A Day Filled With Choices

"Come to the table. I love you with a love everlasting. A love that is steady and true and personal for you. I desire to give you your desires. They are a gift from Me to be uncovered and recovered. I am the hope that cannot be diminished. Hope in Me. I care about what concerns you, because I care about you. You are on My mind and in My heart. I have prepared the way for you to go. You have not been this way before. It will be alright. See I want to give you more. Open your heart and mind to receive. I want the best for you. Choose this day to believe."

*"When I called, you answered me; you
greatly emboldened me.."*
Psalm 138:3 NIV

The Way Made Bold

"I delight in you. Your presence brings Me pleasure. You are
My protected treasure. I have given you everything you need.
I will continue to do so because we are family. We are one,
you and I. Come, let us change the world upside down. Let us
make an impact for My glory. It will be played out in the midst
of your story. With your gifts and talents and skills practiced,
you will see Me at work in your life. You will see that I am the
one who speaks peace into your strife. I am the Prince of Peace
and I rule and reign over your heart and life as you invite Me
in. Engage in the walking out of My best for you. I am leading
you forth in greatness. I am leading you forth in boldness. As
you bring Me into your day-to-day activities, you will see how
I show up to shift the atmosphere. You are My atmosphere
shifter. You bring Me with you wherever you go. You will speak
words and take actions that will change hearts and lives for My
glory. I am with you always. Remember you are not alone. In
you, I have found My home."

"After the earthquake came a fire, but the Lord
was not in the fire. And after the fire
came a gentle whisper."
1 Kings 19:12 NIV

I Am Speaking Always

"I am speaking still. Whether in the sun or rain, My truth will rise to the surface again. When you cannot hear clearly, quiet yourself from the inside out. Sometimes I speak in a whisper, other times in a shout. If you are eager to hear and quick to listen, you will know the truth that I share with My own. You are My own. You belong to Me. I will show you right where you fit. The table has been set. Your place has been set apart. No one else can take your place. I have given you the grace. I have given you the power you need to accomplish what I planned for you to do. I do not give you assignments with the intent to fail. I want the best for you forever and always. Lean into Me. Learn from Me and go forth in boldness and confidence and power. I am here with you this very hour."

"Every good and perfect gift is from above,
coming down from the Father of the heavenly
lights, who does not change like
shifting shadows."
James 1:17 NIV

A Light With No Shadow

"I have come to restore that which was broken. I have come to bring hope in the center of your doubt. I am the light that shifts your atmosphere. I establish your steps and make the way clear. You will know the next step to take. Come, let us rise together. The time has come to awake. Awake to the greatness of Me that lies in the deepest of you. I am calling you forth to shine. Do not worry about exposure. In the transparency of you, others see Me. It is Me in you that causes others to marvel. There is power in you you do not yet see. It is released when you allow Me to be Me, by you being you. You are your most powerful when you are engaging with Me; we partner together to change trajectories. Hand in hand, together we go. The true impact of growth, you may never know."

"Though you have not seen him, you love him;
and even though you do not see him now,
you believe in him and are filled with an
inexpressible and glorious joy."
1 Peter 1:8 NIV

Joy Unspeakable

"I am alive forevermore. I am the way. I am the one who has gone before. I have made a way of hope in the wilderness of doubt. The battle is won. I have gone up with a shout. Fear no longer has a say. Love is here to stay. I am opening your eyes to see and your ears to hear. I am the one who makes the way clear. I fill you with peace unshakeable and joy unspeakable. I am the one who sees, hears and cares. I am the one beyond compare. You are the joy of My heart. There is never a day when we are apart. I will confirm My word to you. Get ready to receive."

"If the ax is dull and its edge unsharpened, more
strength is needed but skill will bring success."
Ecclesiastes 10:10 NIV

Skills for Success

"I have given you more than you need to succeed. Trust that I have given you gifts, talents and abilities. Do not compare to another. Choose to seek Me instead for ways to use and develop the gifts I have given. They are for others. Others have need of what you have to offer. If you do not know what you have to offer, Ask Me. I will show you the wonder of who you are. You will see the wonder of Me in what you do and say. You have entered into covenant with Me. Rejoice, watch, and pray. Hear what I will say. Do what I instruct. I have given you a heart to obey. It is your smile that makes My day. Do you know how beautiful you are? I love you more than you think I do. I am opening your heart to receive the love I have. Rejoice this day. Know you make My heart glad."

"The Lord makes firm the steps of the
one who delights in him"
Psalm 37:23 NIV

Your Steps Are Settled

"I have given you the hope of promise fulfilled. I do not speak a word for it to not come to pass. I am your anchor. I am the place where you can rest safe and solid. I have set your feet upon the rock of Me. I have set your path and established your steps. I give you encouragement and direction to go in the way I instruct. I do not leave you without a plan. I do not leave you without a team. We are in this together. You are never alone. I am your resting place. You are My home. I am calling you alongside Me to do mighty exploits for My glory. Others will look and marvel at our story. They will see Me at work in you. They will know that you are Mine and I am yours. It has been set up as an eternal covenant from day one. Believe in Me and the truth I speak. The best is yet to come. I have called you strong, not weak. You are powerful in Me. Much more than you know. Ask Me for direction. I will show you where to go."

*"Ask me, and I will make the nations your
inheritance, the ends of the earth
your possession."*
Psalm 2:8, NIV

Simply Ask

"I have released you to rejoice. I have set you free from that which has held you back. You are no longer bound to fear and lack. I have given you all you need and more. Arise, acknowledge and ask. I am here and I am up for the task. Do not be afraid to ask Me what you truly want. I know your heart. I know what is best. I am the God of peace and rest. Rest in the knowledge that I am here, and I am for you. I am the one on the scene. I am at work on your behalf. I have conquered so you can conquer. I have won so you can win. You are called alongside Me to engage in the victory. Be not afraid to gather the spoils. I have released you to rejoice in the fruits of your labor."

"Before I formed you in the womb I knew you,
before you were born I set you apart; I appointed
you as a prophet to the nations."
Jeremiah 1:5, NIV

Known From the Beginning

"You are not the average person. I have called you beyond the status quo. You are My original; My one-and-only. There is no other quite like you. See and embrace that which makes you unique. I love you uniquely. I have given you gifts all your own, however, they are not for you alone. Your gifts are to show others who I am. To show them they are not alone and that I do care. I care for you and others so deeply. The depth of My love cannot be adequately expressed. The depths in Me call to the depths in you. Come forth and join Me in exploring who you are and who I am in you. You will know I am yours and you are Mine. I am for you, not against you. You are free to seek Me and know Me. The choice is yours. It has always been. My promises to you are yes and amen."

"For no matter how many promises God has made, they are 'Yes' in Christ. And so through him the 'Amen' is spoken by us to the glory of God."
2 Corinthians 1:20, NIV

The Answer Is Yes and Amen

"It is My presence that goes before you and makes the way straight. I am bringing clarity in the midst of confusion. I am making the way clear. You will know I am here. You will know that I do care. I do listen. I do hear. I am nearer to you than you know. Ask Me to show you the nearness of Me. I will give you eyes to see. I have called you forth in hope this day. I am the answer to the prayers you pray. That which you ask of Me in My name shall be done. I am the God who stays. I do not run. Nothing you can say or do can change My love for you. It is a done deal. My mind has been made. I am your shelter and shade. I am your provider and protector. You are My vector; My desired target. You are the joy set before Me. You are that reason for what I do. You are that treasured; you, yes, you."

"When enemies come in like a flood, the Spirit of the Lord will put them to flight"
Isaiah 59:19, NIV

Raise the Standard of Victory Won

"I am calling you forth. Do you hear the sound? You are the solution others have been looking and waiting for. As you acknowledge My presence in your midst, you will see the solution arise. It has been there all along; hidden to be revealed. Victory is assured. The foe is defeated. Arise to advance. Engage in the dance. Your song is playing. Go on, take the chance. I give you eyes to see the provision. Do not despise the small beginning. Plant and trust that what springs forth, I bring forth. The harvest is up to Me. The planting is up to you. Watch in wonder and see what I will do."

The King's Riches ©2017

*"I will instruct you and teach you in the way you
should go; I will counsel you with my
loving eye on you."*
Psalm 32:8, NIV

I Show You the Way

"There is no fear of lack when you know your connections. I
have called you alongside Me and have given you provision
already. Follow where I lead, being confident that you have
everything you need. What is it you think you lack? Ask of
Me. I have your back. I lead you forth in the way to go. I have
called you to adventure with Me. Lean into Me. Rest assured I
am at the helm. Look to Me and be loosed of overwhelm. I am
the beginning. I am the end. You are the one I have chosen as
friend. You have a choice to choose Me in return. I am patient
with you. There is much to learn. I am teaching you who I am
and who you are. You are My priceless jewel. You are My rising
star."

"If you remain in me and my words remain in you, ask whatever you wish, and it will be done for you."
John 15:7, NIV

My Words Come to Pass

"I am the anchor of your soul. I reveal to you that you are whole. You are enough and not too much. You will know My healing touch. I have given you hopes and dreams for My plans and purposes. They will come to fruition as you lean into Me. Learn of Me and My ways. I have counted your hairs and established your steps. Every detail has been thought of, nothing left to chance. Take My hand and join Me in the dance. The cadence of My heart beats for you. I am forever faithful. I am forever true. I settle the troubled mind as it is focused on Me. You are My beloved one. Arise and see."

"Therefore go and make disciples of all nations,
baptizing them in the name of the Father and
of the Son and of the Holy Spirit, and teaching
them to obey everything I have commanded you.
And surely I am with you always, to
the very end of the age."
Matthew 28:19-20, NIV

With You Always

"I have gifted you with My presence. I am always here for the receiving; always here for the enjoying. I love when you acknowledge My presence. It means you see Me. You care to take time to enter into the rest of Me. I long to have you sit and rest in My presence. This is where strength and joy are found. This is where your cup is filled afresh. I am He who rescues and redeems you. I am God who took on flesh. I have come to show you rest. I reveal to you that which is most important. I give you the strength to carry out My plans for you. You are not alone. I have gathered others alongside. You are My joy. You are My pride. You are called to shine, not hide."

"See, I am doing a new thing! Now it springs up; do you not perceive it? I am making a way in the wilderness and streams in the wasteland."
Isaiah 43:19, NIV

Rivers in the Desert

"My promises shall spring forth. My words will come to pass. I do not speak a thing without the power to make it so. You have waited and wondered and even wandered, but I am bringing you back to Me. I am reminding you of that which I promised you. I am on the scene. I have not left, nor have I forgotten. You will see what you hoped for come to pass. My glory shall pass before your eyes. Get ready for a holy surprise. I have been here all along and I am giving you eyes to see. Your heart is open and ready to receive. Today is the day of promise. Victory is assured. I am the God of the possible. I am true to My word."

*"Why spend money on what is not bread, and
your labor on what does not satisfy? Listen,
listen to me, and eat what is good, and you will
delight in the richest of fare."*
Isaiah 55:2, NIV

True Riches that Satisfy

"I go before you and lead the way. I draw you forth and desire you to stay. I have much to show you, much to tell. I am known by you and I know you well. I know your thoughts before you think them and yet I ask you to share. I want to hear what you have to say. I care about what concerns you. I am the hope you have been looking for. I am your anchor. I am your door. I give you full access to Me at any time. I will fill you to the full and it will not cost you a dime. The goodness of Me is yours for the receiving. The price has been paid. I have deemed you worthy. Worthy to believe in, worthy to delight in. You are My delight. You are My joy. Believe. Receive. Rejoice."

"You open your hand and satisfy the desires
of every living thing."
Psalm 145:16, NIV

Never-ending Supply

"I am the God of increase. I am the God of more. I am the the way. I am the door. I have provided your supply, even when the well feels dry. You are the one I look protect. I see you even when you think you are invisible. You are not alone. There are more for you than against you. I will show you those who fight alongside with you. You have gifts, talents , and provisions others need. Plant the seed I have given and stand amazed at the harvest. The fullness of time comes. Watch and be ready. You do your part and I do Mine. That is the way of love divine."

"Your eyes saw my unformed body; all the days
ordained for me were written in your book
before one of them came to be."
Psalm 139:16, NIV

By Design

"I have given you the gift of Me. I am the one who has set you free. I have designed you and My plans and purposes for you on purpose. Ask Me to reveal Myself to you, and I will. I invite you into relationship and adventure with Me. I am calling you near so you can hear and see. See that I am for you, that I have more for you than you can think or imagine. I am calling you into a paradigm shift. A new way of thinking and seeing and speaking. You will speak forth that which I show you. I watch over My word to perform it. I will do what I said I would. I am forever trustworthy and good."

*"And we all, who with unveiled faces contemplate
the Lord's glory, are being transformed into his
image with ever-increasing glory, which comes
from the Lord, who is the Spirit"*
2 Corinthians 3:18, NIV

Transformation

"It is in fellowship with Me that you are made free. I am the one who reveals Myself to you. I also reveal yourself to you. You are My masterpiece. I love to watch you progress. You shine brightest when you allow Me access to you. When you invite Me into your present, I can heal your past and show you your true future. I have made grand plans for you who is near and dear to My heart. You are the apple of My eye. I have allowed you access to Me at any time. I am your supply. I am the well that never runs dry. My Spirit within gives you the power you need to succeed. You do not go alone. I am revealing your team to you, your band of brothers. It takes a family. You all need each other. Go forth together as one."

*"You turned my wailing into dancing; you
removed my sackcloth and clothed me with joy,
that my heart may sing your praises and not be
silent. Lord my God, I will praise you forever."*
Psalm 30:11-12, NIV

Dancing into Victory

"I have turned your mourning into dancing. I have turned your sorrow into joy. You have come a long way. Receive the fruits of your labor. Rejoice in the victory that has been provided for you. Receive the spoils. Embrace the treasure others are. I have given you a growing capacity to enrich the lives of many. Receive that you may give. You are a channel of hope, a conduit of My love, and a catapult of My peace. My peace in your heart is evidence of My Spirit working in you. As you allow Me to bless you, you can be a greater blessing to others. Flow in the freedom I give. Let nothing hold you back from that which I have called you into. I have set you apart and sent you forth. You do not go alone. I am with you at every turn. You are the one I have called on adventure. Venture forth with joy!"

"My beloved spoke and said to me, 'Arise, my darling, my beautiful one, come with me.'"
Song of Songs 2:10, NIV

Rise Up and Come Near

"I awaken your senses to the nearness of Me. I am the door that is open for you. I have given you full access to Me. Whatever you need I am here to provide. You are a light meant to shine, not hide. Do not hide in the shadows of doubt, fear and lack. Rise up, My Love, know that I have your back. When you rise and shine and be who you are, others will see Me near and far. I am your defense. I am your healer. I am your guide and faithful leader. I am the one who has designed not only the plan, but you. Ask Me if you do not know what to do. I will answer. Trust that you hear. Come closer still. You will know I am near."

*"For the revelation awaits an appointed time;
it speaks of the end and will not prove false.
Though it linger, wait for it; it will certainly
come and will not delay."*
Habakkuk 2:3, NIV

My Word Comes to Pass

"There is a fullness of time; a time when that which I have spoken comes to pass. Believe the words I speak are true. They are weightier than the lies that try to crowd out truth. Light has spoken and will continue to speak. I am the light and I have placed My light within you, that you should go forth and proclaim that which I have done. Speak forth that which I will do. I am forever faithful and forever true. I have given you everything you need already. Practice the gifts I have given. Though they seem small, the potential for growth is not lost. I will give you opportunities to practice. I will make you sensitive to My Spirit if you ask. You were born for this. I have made you ready for the task."

"See, I have engraved you on the palms of my hands; your walls are ever before me."
Isaiah 49:16, NIV

Always Remembered

"Ask Me the thoughts I think toward you. I love you more than you can imagine, and yet, I am expanding your capacity for more. I have more for you that you have not walked in yet. Get ready to receive what I have for you. It is yours, and it is good. I am a good, good Father who gives good, good gifts to My own. That is you, My Love. You are My own. You are not forgotten. You are very much remembered. You are on My mind and in My heart more than you realize. Ask Me to show you how I see you. You are not used to seeing yourself through My eyes. As you look to Me, I will align your vision. I will establish your steps. I will guide you with My eye upon you. You are the one I desire to be with. Make no mistake, you are a delight. You are the joy of My heart. I am your hope. I cause your doubt to take flight. Come with Me and let us explore the highest of heights. The view is spectacular and the company is breathtaking!"

*"We are therefore Christ's ambassadors, as
though God were making his appeal through us.
We implore you on Christ's behalf:
Be reconciled to God."*
2 Corinthians 5:20, NIV

Ambassadors of Influence

"I have made you fluent in the language of Me. The more you set time aside to acknowledge and be with Me, the more you will learn to speak like I speak and think like I think. We influence and are influenced by those we spend time with. This is both exciting and sobering. Yes, you have the power and responsibility of influence. Others are noticing and taking note. What is the truth waiting for you to share? You are the proof that shows others I care. Lean into Me and learn My ways. I fill you with calm and confidence. I give you the power and opportunity to carry out My plan for you. I order your days and establish your steps. I reveal to you the way to go. Ask Me what you need to know. I have given you full access to Me. I am here eternally."

"So God created mankind in his own image, in the image of God he created them; male and female he created them."
Genesis 1:27, NIV

Image-bearers of Love

"I am the One who overcomes. I am the One who overshadows. I am the light that dispels the darkness. Darkness and fear cannot hide in the light of My love. I have called you to do the same. You carry My Spirit. You bear My image and name. You are the one I have given My influence to. Go and share. Influence and increase are yours for the implementing. I exalt the humble. I give grace to those who are surrendered to Me. Those who acknowledge My presence and invite Me into their world. I am here always. If you ask Me to reveal Myself to you even further, I will. I watch over My word to perform it. Confidence is enhanced by confirmation. Ask and you will receive. Advance My cause and so cause others to believe. It is Me working in conjunction with you. We are in this together. Those joined together are stronger than they could ever be apart. We bear the same image, we share the same heart."

"Before I formed you in the womb I knew you,
before you were born I set you apart; I appointed
you as a prophet to the nations."
Jeremiah 1:5, NIV

Chosen from the Start

"I am love, hope, and peace eternal. I am here always and forever. There is never a time when I am not without you. Nothing can separate you from Me. It is a choice I have made from before the beginning. I have chosen you from before you began. I decided to love you sight unseen, and yet I have always seen you. I have always loved you. As you begin to acknowledge My love for you, you will be open to receiving all the more. I have set a love in your heart. I have chosen you to call My home. I am revealing to you My goodness. I am revealing to you, your loveliness. Yes, you are My dwelling place. You are all together lovely. See you as I see you. Love you as I love you. It is a journey worth pursuing. It is an adventure worth embarking on. You shine brighter than the sun."

"Pray also for me, that whenever I speak, words may be given me so that I will fearlessly make known the mystery of the gospel,"
Ephesians 6:19, NIV

Speak with Boldness

"Take time to bask in the light of My love. It is the light of My love that causes you to shine. You are the one I have chosen. You are the one to follow My lead and watch others take heed. I have given you words to speak that others need to hear. Speak them with boldness, confidence, grace and love. I am more than sufficient. I am more than enough. I call you alongside Me to partner with Me; you and I together. You are qualified. You are worthy. You have what it takes to make an immeasurable impact on those you come in contact with. I have given you all you need. Do not despise the seed."

The King's Riches ©2017

"But you will receive power when the Holy Spirit comes on you; and you will be my witnesses in Jerusalem, and in all Judea and Samaria, and to the ends of the earth."
Acts 1:8, NIV

The Spirit's Power to Propel

"You have sought Me and found Me. I am but a mere whisper away. I am always listening to what you say. I have given you a holy boldness to ask for what you most desire. I know what it is I have for you. When you move in faith and ask for what you want, you come into agreement and alignment with Me. We are in this together. Me in you and you in Me; working together in unity. I call you forth into the new I have for you. Take My hand and take a step forward into My best. My Spirit within gives you the power to move into what I have set aside for you. You are My workmanship created for good works. You are My treasure, My masterpiece. You are the one I delight to display. I have given you a hope that never fades away. I have given you a love that is yours to embrace. Look up and let your eyes see the love with which I love you. You are Mine. You are the one I have decided on before you ever feel qualified. It is not what you have done but what we can do together. Together we change lives."

*"Those who look to him are radiant; their faces
are never covered with shame."*
Psalm 34:5, NIV

True Radiance

"I am the one who has gone before. I am your hope. I am your door. You will see the way marked ahead for you. I have gone before and paved the way. I have come to set your fears at bay. No longer in doubt and dread shall you dwell. I have taken your shame. I know you too well. I know who I have called you to be. Take a step and embrace your free. Hear the words I speak to you. You are breathtaking and radiant. No other will do. No other can do what I have uniquely designed you to do. Look forward to Me. See where I lead. Join the cavalcade of victors. Embrace and enter into all I have for you. Know that you are safe with Me. You are safe with Me as we journey to the unknown. You are the one I look at and am home."

"But the Lord said to me, "Do not say, 'I am too young.' You must go to everyone I send you to and say whatever I command you. 8 Do not be afraid of them, for I am with you and will rescue you," declares the Lord."
Jeremiah 1:7-8, NIV

Delivered Out of Fear

"There is no room for fear. I am your deliverer and I am here. I give you the words to speak when you feel you have nothing to say. I reveal Myself to you, afresh and anew each day. You will see Me at work when you invite Me into your day. Involve Me in your life; the joy as well as the strife. When you allow Me access, you will see that I have allowed you access to Me. What is Mine is yours. Receive and be blessed. In Me, you will find sacred rest. Yes, there is sacredness to rest. It rejuvenates and refreshes. Come and sit a spell. Take a breath. All is well. It will be ok. You will see Me there. I do hear. You do matter. I do care."

"Before they call I will answer; while they
are still speaking I will hear."
Isaiah 65:24, NIV

Ask and I Will Answer

"I am here regardless. Regardless if you acknowledge Me or not.
I am always here. You can choose how near you come. I will
not reject you as you have feared. I will set those fears to flight.
I will align your thoughts to Mine as you shift your sight. Look
to Me to see as I see. I am opening your ears to hear what I
am speaking to you. You will hear Me more and more as your
desire to hear Me grows. The more you hear, the more you
will want to hear. I have much to share with you. It delights
My heart to hear you ask Me what I am speaking to you. Rest
assured, I will answer. I will surprise you. It is what I do. I love
to see the look of joy and anticipation in your eyes. You bring
Me much delight just by being you. You do not have to perform
for Me. I see you as I have designed you to be and I call you
forth. Trust Me in all things; especially in the things for which
you are unsure. Your doubts have no room when hope has filled
your heart. I am hope eternal. I was and am and ever will be. I
am your compass. Follow Me."

*"My Father's house has many rooms; if that were
not so, would I have told you that I am going
there to prepare a place for you? And if I go and
prepare a place for you, I will come back and
take you to be with me that you also
may be where I am."*
John 14:2-3, NIV

A Space Prepared

"The time for the singing of the birds has come. The battle has been fought, and the victory won. I have given you the spoils. It is for you. It is for your receiving. I open My hand and satisfy your desires. Receive the love I have poured forth for you. It is especially for you. You are not an afterthought, you are not a leftover. You are the guest of honor. I have prepared My best for you. The table has been set and your seat is marked by your name. I have given you a place that is tailor-made for you. If you do not enjoy it, it does not get enjoyed. I have given you gifts for the glory of My name. Do not bury your talents in fear and shame. It is My Spirit, My power that works in you to do that which is excellent. Go forth in My grace. Go forth in the power I provide. Choose this day to shine, not hide."

"By faith Abraham, when called to go to a place
he would later receive as his inheritance, obeyed
and went, even though he did not know
where he was going."
Hebrews 11:8, NIV

Uncharted Territory

"I see you follow Me to places you have not been. It does not feel familiar because it is not familiar. Yet, you trust Me. You are trust My leading. Lean into Me. Learn from Me and I will take you places you could not dare to imagine. I want more for you than you think is possible. I am expanding your thinking and shifting your paradigm. You will think as I think and see as I see, when you spend time with Me. In our relationship there is an ebb and flow; a speaking of ones heart and a listening to what is being communicated, verbally and nonverbally. I am showing you who I am and revealing to you who you are. You are My priceless jewel and I, your bright and Morning star! Together we shine much brighter than you ever could apart. You and I are one. We share the same heart."

"Since ancient times no one has heard, no ear has perceived, no eye has seen any God besides you, who acts on behalf of those who wait for him."
Isaiah 64:4, NIV

Revealed Strength

"I have given you the direction you seek. See yourself as I see you. I see you are strong, not weak. You have more power in you than you have fully realized. I am at work on your behalf for you to both know and grow in this power that you carry. It has been there all along, but past circumstances and the lies held therein, have kept you bound. I will reveal Myself to you in increasingly new ways. I will reveal yourself to you, as well. I do not reveal yourself to you to berate you. Instead I reveal to you the power I have given to move forth in. I reveal to heal. That which I shed My light on is that which I can heal, if you let Me. I have given you the power to see the truth in the midst of the lie that surrounded it. The truth has more power than the lie could ever hope to have. Come to Me, and let My Spirit apply the healing salve."

*"But we have this treasure in jars of clay to show
that this all-surpassing power is from
God and not from us."*
2 Corinthians 4:7, NIV

Carrier of My Presence

"It is to you, I belong. It is to Me, your heart sings its song; a song of freedom, hope and deliverance. Though you did not know the way before, I am making things clear. I am causing things to make sense. You can see Me at work in your life and circumstances. You know that I see, I hear and I care. My love for you is beyond compare. Do not compare My love to another. That is a waste of time. Just receive and enjoy. Rest in the knowledge that I am yours and you are Mine. I have given you what you need for life and godliness. I have enriched you with joy and happiness. Revel in the gift of My love so free. I am opening your ears to hear and your eyes to see. See that the glory that rests upon Me, is also upon you. You are a carrier of My presence. You bring Me into your everyday life. You speak My peace in the midst of strife. You show others that they, too, belong. You realize I am with you forever; I have been here all along."

*"This is what the Lord says—your Redeemer, the
Holy One of Israel: 'I am the Lord your God, who
teaches you what is best for you, who directs
you in the way you should go.'"*
Isaiah 48:17, NIV

Skilled to Succeed

"I am giving you tools to be successful. I will make your way
prosperous. When you are not sure of strategies, ask Me. I
will share My heart and secrets with you. I am giving you
what you need to profit. Plant the seed I give and tend to it in
faithfulness. You will see it grow. Make no mistake, that which
you entrust to Me can be trusted. Rest assured I take what
you give Me and multiply it for your benefit and the benefits
of those around you. You are not alone. What you do is not
just for you. Others are impacted by the steps you take. Look
around, My love, we leave a fabulous wake. Trust that the
results will come as the planting is done. You do your part and I
do Mine, That is the rhythm of love divine."

"The tongue has the power of life and death, and those who love it will eat its fruit."
Proverbs 18:21, NIV

Power of Life in the Tongue

"I have given you the power to speak life into your situations, into the situations of others. I will give you the words to speak if you ask. In so asking, take courage to speak the words you hear. You have the power to bring Me front and center. To show others Me when all they see is trouble and fear. Your obedience brings Me near. I can work with a heart tender toward Me. I will show you and you will see. I have given you the power of living free. Free from fear, doubt and shame. I am that which you need exactly when you need it. I am the one who shows you where you fit. Believe in Me and the power I have to make a difference. I am leading you forth into the more I have for you. Trust in My love given especially to you. You are My chosen one. No other can do what you can do."

*"God has ascended amid shouts of joy, the Lord
amid the sounding of trumpets."*
Psalm 47:5, NIV

Follow the Breaker into Breakthrough

"I am in the midst of you. I have not left. I am still at work for your highest good. I will reveal to you where I am. You always have and will always be part of the plan. I will show you where you fit. You will know this is it. Seek Me and you will find Me. Search for Me with all your heart. Trust that I am at work. Trust that I know what I am doing. My hope is here and it springs eternal. Watch it spring forth. It is quite a sight. I am giving you truth to chase away doubt. I am the Breaker who has gone up with a shout."

"He has filled them with skill to do all kinds of work as engravers, designers, embroiderers in blue, purple and scarlet yarn and fine linen, and weavers—all of them skilled workers and designers."
Exodus 35:35, NIV

Skilled Master Craftsman

"Watch and see Me do wonders among you. I am on the move and I move on your behalf. I have equipped you with the tools you need to succeed. Practice your skills faithfully and you will see growth exponentially. I have gifted you with My presence. You do not go alone. Adventure is best when joined together. I have called you to be set apart, not separated. Be extraordinary, not ordinary. I have given you those who will help you achieve the greatness within. I am adding to your team those that best serve the cause of Me. I have anointed you and have set you free. You are free to explore the land laid out just for you. Inhabit your inheritance. Help others to inhabit theirs. We are in this together. I am faithful. I am forever."

*"Take my yoke upon you and learn from me, for
I am gentle and humble in heart, and you will
find rest for your souls."*
Matthew 11:29, NIV

Lightness of My Love

"My yoke is easy and My burden is light. I have caused your fears to take flight. No longer are you held beneath the crushing weight of fear. Look up, My Love, and know I am here. I am in the midst of you leading you in My way. I have come to release you from that which has held you bound. You are hidden in Me. There is no fear of Me losing sight of you. I guide you with My eye upon you and I lead you in the way you should go. I am here where I have always been: right by your side. You are meant to shine, not hide. I have given you a light that will shine brighter than you realize. Follow where I lead and get ready for surprise!"

*"Why, my soul, are you downcast? Why so
disturbed within me? Put your hope in God, for I
will yet praise him, my Savior and my God."*
Psalm 43:5, NIV

Hope in Me

"I have created you for more. I am showing you what that more is. Ask Me to help you see and know. I will show you the way to go. I am filling you with the hope that you have not dared to hope for. I am the hope you have been longing for. I am the joy unspeakable and full of glory. I am the author of your story. I am the one who has invited you into the dance. I am the one who has given you a second chance. Your story is not finished. The pages continue on. I have called you into greatness for My glory. You are the one I have chosen. You are the one I love. Peace, be still. I am setting in order that which has been in chaos. I am the Prince of Peace. My reign will never cease."

"Pray also for me, that whenever I speak, words may be given me so that I will fearlessly make known the mystery of the gospel,"
Ephesians 6:19, NIV

Speak Forth in Boldness

"I have given you what you need for the task at hand. Your provision has already been provided to you. Ask Me to show you the details and I will. I will show you what you must do. I will instruct you with My eye upon you. As you look to Me you will see how I am revealing Myself to you. You are a solution. You bring answers to those who have questions. You have great impact and influence on others. Even if I give you a word to speak that does not make sense to you, your obedience in speaking it will open others to see Me in ways they have not seen before. I am a personal God who relates personally to My people. I have blessed you to be a blessing. You have what you need to go forth with confidence and boldness. You know you are not alone. I go with you and cheer you on. I believe in you and the gift I have placed within. You, My Love, are born to win."

"Have I not commanded you? Be strong and courageous. Do not be afraid; do not be discouraged, for the Lord your God will be with you wherever you go."
Joshua 1:9, NIV

Strong and Courageous

"I am the one who fights for you on your behalf. I am your deliverer. I am your freedom fighter. I am the one who knows the end from the beginning. You and I, we have a history of winning. I will reveal to you the spoils that are yours. Take courage to walk through the open doors. You have not been this way before. Stick with Me and get ready to explore. Explore the more I have for you. Know the richness of My love and the lavishness that I pour it out with. I am revealed in the whisper. I am rejoiced in the shout. You belong. You fit in. Let there be no doubt. I have given you direction. I have shown you the way. Your seed has been planted. Your harvest is near. Expand your borders. I fill you with cheer."

*"And without faith it is impossible to please God,
because anyone who comes to him must believe
that he exists and that he rewards those
who earnestly seek him."*
Hebrews 11:6, NIV

Reward of Love

"I delight in the light of you. I delight in the light in your eyes. Get ready to receive the surprise. I long to surprise you with My love. Just when you think I am not noticing or I did not hear your cry. I see the smile on your face and hear you ask, 'why?' The answer is always the same: because I love you. Love is My name. It is the very nature of Me. I am opening your eyes so you can see. Enter into that which I have set apart just for you. To receive that which is yours, you first must believe it is. I am the rewarder of those that diligently seek Me. You do not diligently seek that which you first do not believe. I am changing your paradigms. As you shift your focus you will see the path marked straight. Go forth in confidence. I have clothed you in My righteousness."

"You, God, are awesome in your sanctuary; the God of Israel gives power and strength to his people. Praise be to God!"
Psalm 68:35, NIV

God of Wonders

"Do not doubt the gift I have given. Do not doubt the gift you are. You are My anointed one. You are meant to go far. You have much influence and impact. Not for your sake, but for Mine. I am the light that causes you to shine. Step out into the more I have for you. Be it a baby step or a leap. I will give you ears to hear the words I speak. Take courage and know that you are strong, not weak. Your power is reflective of My Spirit working in you. We are partners together on this adventure. I call you forth as I created you. Trust Me that I have a different vantage point. I am giving you a fresh perspective. You will see things from different angles and solutions will arise. I am the God of wonders. I am the God of surprise."

"Two are better than one, because they have a
good return for their labor."
Ecclesiastes 4:9, NIV

Better Together

"I am here in the midst of you. I am opening your eyes to see. The shackles of fear that once had bound you, are loosed. You are indeed free. I am calling you forth to go with Me. Go where you could not go alone. I have designed it this way. You can go so much further and do so much more with Me, than you can ever do without. I am at the helm. I have charted the course. I know the way because I am the way. Trust that I will get us there safely. Turbulence may arise, but never stop looking at My eyes. With your gaze on Me, you will rise and do what you didn't dare think possible. With your eyes on the waves, they will overcome you. The choice is yours. It is a continuous choosing. I am the constant that is ever present. I am not leaving your side. Take courage and soar. You are not meant to hide. You were created for more."

*"So Christ himself gave the apostles, the prophets,
the evangelists, the pastors and teachers, to
equip his people for works of service, so that the
body of Christ may be built up until we all reach
unity in the faith and in the knowledge of the
Son of God and become mature, attaining to the
whole measure of the fullness of Christ."*
Ephesians 4:11-13, NIV

Benefits of Maturity

"With your eyes focused on Me, you will begin to see. You will see that I am at work. I am moving, even when you feel as if circumstances are standing still. Be faithful in the little and I will make you ruler over much. Notice your focus is on what I have set before you to do. The outcome is up to Me. There are benefits that come from maturity; responsibilities to guard and protect that which I have given. You are worthy because you are Mine. I polish you so you will shine. Embrace the cleansing that I offer. You will feel fresh and emerge renewed; ready for the task at hand. I am preparing you to receive your land."

*"The boundary lines have fallen for me in
pleasant places; surely I have a
delightful inheritance."*
Psalm 16:6, NIV

Borders of Inheritance

"I have come near to reveal to you I am here. I will reveal Myself
to you in undeniable ways; not only for your comfort, but also
for your assurance. You will know that I created space just for
us. I am never too busy and you are never unimportant for
Me to take notice of you. I guide you with My eye upon you.
You rest in the palm of My hand. Trust Me to lead you to your
land. It is for you; tailor-made and chosen specifically for you.
Choose to see and believe and enter into that which I have
laid aside for you. You have a rich inheritance in Me that is
meant to be enjoyed presently. Each day is a gift waiting to be
unwrapped. Go ahead and open it, it is yours. I have not made
a mistake. I have thought of every detail. You and I are meant to
prevail."

"Let us hold unswervingly to the hope we profess,
for he who promised is faithful."
Hebrews 10:23, NIV

Faithful and True

"Interact with My word, and so connect with Me. Hear what I am saying and see what I am doing. I am at work in your life and on your behalf. That which I do, I do completely. I will do what I say I will do. Trust is the key that brings My word to pass. Trust that I am faithful and true. I will prove Myself strong on your behalf. You will know that I care. There is no detail too small that I don't think about. No ask too big that I cannot handle. You and your requests are not insignificant. You carry more significance and influence than you realize. It is not for your glory, but Mine. Therefore be done hiding. Come into My light and shine. You have gifts worth sharing. You have words worth speaking; doubt no longer. It is My hope that makes you stronger."

*"The Lord has done great things for us, and we
are filled with joy."*
Psalm 126:3, NIV

Filled with Joy

"I have called you to greater. I have called you for more. I have called you to excel. I have called you to soar. You are Mine and I am yours. You were bought with a price. I would do it all again, but once sufficed. You are the joy that has been set before Me. You were the prize I was after. You are first place. Yes, you. You who only have known last place, I call you chosen and sought after. You fill My heart with joy and My mouth with laughter. I delight in the light of you. Others see My glory, too. You shine brightest and best when you flow in the gifts I have given. You are worth pursuing and your skills are worth practicing. Take care to develop and share the gifts within. Start where you are. That is where to begin."

"The Lord appeared to us in the past saying: 'I have loved you with an everlasting love; I have drawn you with unfailing kindness.'"
Jeremiah 31:3, NIV

You Are Loved

"I am here in the midst of you. I have been here all along. I am giving you eyes to see how I am working in your situations. I am giving you ears to hear what I am speaking to you. You will know that your conversations with Me are not one sided. Not only do I listen to what you say, but I also speak the answer to what you pray. In this way you will know My heart even more. You will know I am for you, not against you. You will know you have an advocate in Me, not an enemy. I am shifting your paradigms to receive more of Me. Get ready to receive and believe the truth I will reveal to you. It is for your success and for My glory. You will know I am the author of your story. You play an imperative role in the lives of others. You are needed. You are wanted. You are loved."

*"Let us then approach God's throne of grace with
confidence, so that we may receive mercy and
find grace to help us in our time of need."*
Hebrews 4:16, NIV

Humbly Yet Boldly

"Get ready for the influx of My love. My love transforms you from the inside out. It causes you to hope, not doubt. I am filling you with the best of Me, so you can reveal Me to others. Others see Me through you. They are brought to the revelation of Me through your words and actions. Never forget whose you are. You do belong. You do make sense. You do impact others for My glory. You do this by sharing your story and seeing and meeting needs of others. Ask Me to help you see your part. In so seeing, do what I've called you, with the confidence I have called you with. I make you bold with strength in your soul. I give you words to speak that have the power to change lives. Humbly, yet boldly, step out into the more I have for you. It is your inheritance to be enjoyed in the here and now and in the later. I have called you for more. I have called you to greater."

"Taste and see that the Lord is good; blessed is the one who takes refuge in him."
Psalm 34:8, NIV

Taste and See

"I am preparing you for more. Expand your faith. You will see that I watch over My word to perform it. My word comes to pass in the proper way and time. There is not a word I speak that does not come to fruition. I am a keeper of My word and I reveal to you what I am speaking. Take courage to take hold of that which I have laid aside for you. I have given you Me. I am the one who guides you into the more of Me. I will show you what you have not seen before. The way I am leading you have not gone. I am doing a new thing. I lead you forth in favor. Stick close to Me and savor. Savor the presence of Me. Taste and see that I am good. I am worth writing home about, and so are you. Do you have any idea how proud I am of you? In you, I am well pleased. Take rest in the knowledge that you are Mine and I am yours. I will show you more of what that means and looks like. You are precious and priceless and I am causing you to see your worth."

"Though you have not seen him, you love him;
and even though you do not see him now,
you believe in him and are filled with an
inexpressible and glorious joy,"
1 Peter 1:8, NIV

Unspeakable Joy

"I walk forward with you. You do not go alone into the uncharted waters I am calling you to. I have much for you to receive. Open your heart and mind to receive. As you receive the more I have for you, the greater your capacity to give. I am the joy unspeakable you have longed for. I am filling you with My presence. In My presence is peace and fullness of joy. I lead you forth in peace. Do not dismay. Do not despair. I am here. I do care. Trust Me with your triumphs and troubles. I have lifted you out of the pit and dusted you from the rubble. I washed you clean and clothed you in the righteousness of Me. You are My treasured one that I have freed. I saw your need and I have answered. I always have and always will. I loved you then and I love you still."

"As water reflects the face, so one's life
reflects the heart."
Proverbs 27:19, NIV

True Reflection

"It is with kindness and love I draw you forth. I have determined you are one of great worth. I am drawn to such beauty. I see you in Me and I am held captive by you. I am your mirror. I reflect your true beauty back to you. It is not a trick. It is a trust. Trust that I know what I am talking about. I love you first and best, not last and least. You are not an afterthought. You are are a forethought. You have been on My mind and in My heart from before the beginning. I am drawing you forth. Will you allow yourself to go where I lead? It is your choice. It has always your choice. Enter and receive, or not. I believe in you. I believe in the gifts I have given you. As you believe, you will begin to share. As you share, lives are changed. Others will know the hope I have planted within. Take My hand and let us begin."

"My sheep listen to my voice; I know them,
and they follow me."
John 10:27, NIV

Listening to Hear

"I have established your path and I direct your steps. I lead you forth in the way of Me. Listen for My direction, My instructions. I am training your ears to hear Me well. You can hear what I say. I am speaking. Your desire to hear more will take you smack dab in the midst of Me. As you hear and obey, you will hear even more. Listening is a vital part to our relationship. Do not worry that you do not know the end from the beginning. I know and I will reveal to you what you need to know at exactly the right time. You are Mine and you are being aligned. I have shown you the next step. You are free to ask again if you forget. But in your asking and in My reminding you, you do well to do. Do that which I have set before you to do. Work with the spirit of excellence that is yours in Me. Work as the one who has remembered they are free. You are not bound by fear. You are loosed into freedom."

*"In a large house there are articles not only of
gold and silver, but also of wood and clay; some
are for special purposes and some for common
use. Those who cleanse themselves from the
latter will be instruments for special purposes,
made holy, useful to the Master and
prepared to do any good work."*
2 Timothy 2:20-21, NIV

Vessel of Honor

"I have gone before and paved the way. Believe Me, it is good.
I have things set aside for you that you could not even dare
imagine! Will you not join Me and explore our land together?
I have for you an abundance of blessings that you cannot
contain. They are for your enjoyment and sharing. Others have
need of what I have blessed you with. Share freely that which
I have given. You will find yourself filled with unspeakable joy
and full of glory! I am the author of your story. I have written a
masterpiece. I have dusted you off the shelf of invisibility. I have
clothed you in righteousness and placed My glory in you. You
shine brighter than you imagine. When you follow My lead,
you become open to letting Me shine through you. You are My
anointed one and you shine like the sun."

The King's Riches ©2017

"...you also, like living stones, are being built into
a spiritual house to be a holy priesthood, offering
spiritual sacrifices acceptable to God
through Jesus Christ."
1 Peter 2:5, NIV

Lively Stones Meant to Live

"I have given you the gift of Me. I have given you eyes to see. You will look for Me and find Me at work in your everyday life. You will see that I am here, I do care, and I do answer your prayer. You do not go alone. I have called your team alongside you. You will know who they are because they share the same heart. Together you will get the job done. Be open to sharing with those I have called you to. Trust is a solid foundation for the building one up together in love. You are My lively stones built together to achieve great things. Align yourself to that which I have for you. Walk in step and stay on the path. Lean into Me and get ready to receive. Receive that which has already been prepared for you. I give you My best. I love you like that."

*"So if the Son sets you free, you will
be free indeed."*
John 8:36, NIV

Liberty Abounds

"I love you first and best. Where you have strived in your own doing, you are to rest in your own being; being who I created you to be. I see the longing to be free. I will show you that you already are. The choice is yours. You have the ability to go far. I am showing you the open door. Your chains are gone. They are on the floor. You are free to be who I have called you to be. Rise up and come with Me. There is much to be done. Much ground to recover. There is a whole new world to discover. A land that is rich for your enjoyment; My gift to you because I never leave you lacking. Everything I am and have is yours. Ask and receive. I will show you the open doors."

"You make known to me the path of life; you will fill me with joy in your presence, with eternal pleasures at your right hand."
Psalm 16:11, NIV

The Peace of My Presence

"Unwrap the gift of today. Be present in My presence. Receive all I have for you. It is for you to be enjoyed. I love when you relish in the gifts I've given. More so when you settle into the love of the one who gives. My gifts celebrate My love for you. Your gifts are for you and for others, too. I will reveal the recipients. Be on the lookout and be ready to give. I have blessed you to be a blessing. You will recover that which was lost as you uncover that which has been there all along. You do fit. I will show you where you belong."

*"I am the gate; whoever enters through me
will be saved. They will come in and
go out, and find pasture."*
John 10:9, NIV

Door to More

"I reveal Myself to you even though you cannot see Me. I show
you where I am working in your life and where I've worked
in your life before. This gives you faith and courage to see and
believe for more. I am the one who has given you access to Me.
All you have to do is enter into what I have for you. Do not let
fear of making a mistake keep you from approaching Me. I am
more than capable to bringing you back into proper alignment
should you ask amiss. I know your heart and I know what
is best. I am aligning our hearts so they are one in the same.
Expand your borders. Expect Me to move. I am alive and well. I
have set you free to tell. Tell others not to give up hope. I am on
the scene. I see and care and provide for what they need. I am a
good God who cares deeply. The price for your freedom did not
come cheaply. It was worth it, make no mistake. You are worth
it, and so much more. I am your hope. I am the door."

"But now, this is what the Lord says—he who created you, Jacob, he who formed you, Israel: 'Do not fear, for I have redeemed you; I have summoned you by name; you are mine.'"
Isaiah 43:1, NIV

You Are Mine

"I establish your steps and set things in order. I am the God of order and clarity. If you do not know what to do, ask Me. I will gladly reveal Myself and My ways to you. I am calling you forth to greater things in Me. Release fears and doubts that no longer serve. See the best I have for you. I do not just bless others, I bless you, too. Steward well the gifts I give. Others have need of them. You are My treasured one. You are My gem. I polish you by My Spirit as you go and grow with My flow. I have placed within you gifts that only you can do. You are an original. You are not ordinary, you are extraordinary. See the beauty in you and others that has been there all along. I have crafted you in My image and have placed My signature on you. You are Mine. There has been no mistake. I am yours. Today, let us celebrate!"

"See, I am doing a new thing! Now it springs up;
do you not perceive it? I am making a way in the
wilderness and streams in the wasteland."
Isaiah 43:19, NIV

New Things

"I have loved you with an everlasting love. I am the hope
that does not disappoint. I am from forever for forever. I am
revealing Myself to you in fresh, new ways. Seek Me and find
Me. I am hidden to be found. Ask of Me what is on your heart.
I truly want to know. I care about what concerns you. You are
the apple of My eye. You are the one from whom I live and
died. I would do it all again, but once was sufficient. I complete
the work I begin. I know the end from the beginning. I see it,
smile and ask you to join Me on the journey of us. I know that
you are not an island unto yourself. Life is better shared. A
shared life is a life well lived. I am for you. I am for community.
I am the one who knows the design inside and out. I am the
Lord of the Breakthrough and I go up with a shout. It is a shout
that says victory cannot be denied. You are meant to shine, not
hide. You are My glorious and glowing one. The stage has been
set and the battles been won."

"She gave this name to the Lord who spoke to her:
"You are the God who sees me," for she said, "I
have now seen the One who sees me."
Genesis 16:13, NIV

The One Who Sees

"I have forgiven you from the uttermost. Will you forgive yourself? There is much to be done. Much I need you for. Bring your whole self to Me and watch Me restore and renew you. You are made new in Me. You have not been where I am leading you. I am leading you forward in Me. I am causing you to see. See the more I have for you and believe it is yours. I set your feet on the path paved straight. I open doors for you that no man can shut. You have asked and I have answered. Enter and engage in that which is yours. I have not forgotten you. I see you even when you think no one notices. Even when you hope no one notices. You are never far from My gaze. I am here for you always. Your freedom will set others free. You are the one who shines brighter than the sun. It is not about who you are or what you have done. It is about whose you are and what you have in Me. You are more powerful than you realize. Embrace your legacy and follow Me forward."

"As for God, his way is perfect: The Lord's word is flawless; he shields all who take refuge in him."
Psalm 18:30, NIV

The Way Perfect

"I have lead you out of what does not serve you, in order to bring you into what does. Trust that My way is better. My plans are sure and My words are true. I lead you forward into the best I have for you. Receive that which is yours. Engage in the future I have for you. Embrace the preeminence of My presence. I am here always. There is never a time when we are separated. I do not grow tired of you. I love you beyond measure. To be with you is a pleasure. I am the one who has laid the foundation. I have built you up from your very beginning. You are the one I am proud of. You cause My heart to sing with joy. The smile on My face is because of you. Believe you are that cherished. It is as true as the sun. Rejoice in each new day begun."

*"For I am convinced that neither death nor life,
neither angels nor demons, neither the present
nor the future, nor any powers, neither height
nor depth, nor anything else in all creation, will
be able to separate us from the love of God
that is in Christ Jesus our Lord."*
Romans 8:38-39, NIV

Nothing Separates Us

"I am leading you forth in a way you have not gone. Stick close to Me and soldier on. I am your True North. I point you to the way that is straight. I lead you with a heart of love, not hate. Love for My people that few have known. I am calling you forth to show them Me. I have not forgotten. They have always been on My mind and heart; same as you. We are one, we cannot be apart. Nothing can separate you from Me. We are a package deal. Not sold separately. You hold more value than you realize. My love often catches others by surprise. When you are not looking to be loved or valued, behold you find Me. I have been here all along. Your eyes are open to see. Your ears are open to hear. Your heart is open to respond and receive the best I have for you. Believe it is for you. Receive with thanksgiving and rejoice. You are remembered, not forgotten."

"Heal the sick, raise the dead, cleanse those who have leprosy, drive out demons. Freely you have received; freely give."
Matthew 10:8, NIV

Give Liberally

"You will rest in the knowledge that the battle has been won. I am calling you forth to collect the spoils. I have given you instruction. You do not go empty handed. I give you the words to speak and the actions to take. You will know I am speaking to you. I will speak to you in ways you can hear. I know what you will listen to. I created you. I am the one who fashioned you and gifted you to bless others. Share what I have given you. Believe you and your gifts are worth sharing. I know what I am doing. Trust Me to lead you into the best I have for you. Trust by going forth and engaging in the plan I have laid out. I am the one who breaks through with a shout. I lead with a whisper. I am guiding you. To go forward or not is your freedom of choice. I know your heartbeat and I hear your voice. Listen and be willing to engage. I have set you free. Will you leave the cage?"

"The Lord your God is with you, the Mighty
Warrior who saves. He will take great delight in
you; in his love he will no longer rebuke you, but
will rejoice over you with singing."
Zephaniah 3:17, NIV

I Delight in You

"You are Mine and I am yours. I hear you and you hear Me. I am the one who has set you free. You are free to free others. As you move in the freedom that is already yours, you will delight in seeing others embrace their freedom. You are a delight to Me. No matter what you do. I have loved you from the beginning. I will not change My mind. Receive the love I have given. Receive and act in kind. I am the one who influences you to make a difference. You make a difference just by being you. You are free to be you. Take courage to ask the questions to discover and uncover the you that has been there all along. You are worth the discovery and recovery. Never forget. Let the truth of My love change you from the inside out as you yield to Me. I am watching over My word to perform it. It is as good as done. Go forward with Me and see the victory won."

*"He heals the brokenhearted and binds
up their wounds."*
Psalm 147:3, NIV

Healing Hearts

"There is evidence of My presence all around you. I am causing you to awaken to the nearness of Me. I have come to heal the broken hearted and set the oppressed free. You will be guided by My eye. You will hear very clear. I am leading you ever so near. I have given you the direction you seek. I am giving you strength where once you were weak. I am the one who leads you forth into the greater I have for you. Stand still and watch the wonders I will do among you. I am on the move. I am in your midst. Embrace the love I give. Embrace, and do not resist. I am the mighty one who cares. I redeem the time you thought you had lost. You are My precious and priceless one. You are worth the cost. You are worth it and so much more. I am awakening you to adventure. Take courage and explore."

*"For we are God's handiwork, created in Christ
Jesus to do good works, which God prepared
in advance for us to do."*
Ephesians 2:10, NIV

Chosen for Good Works

"I have gifted you to be a solution. You are a solution to many. As you yield to the leading of My Spirit, you will see how you fit. You do belong. You are cared for. There is a role that is tailor made for you. No one else can be who I created you to be. Stop doubting your significance. Stop doubting your gift. Others have need of what I put in you to share. You are unique and beyond compare. You are the one chosen by Me. I am looking at you kid. You are the one I need. I have given you the seed to sow. Plant faithfully and watch how the fruit will grow. Your faithfulness in your acts of faith will ensure others are fed as they are needed. I am giving you the right words to speak at the right time to the right people. Trust that I will get you to where I have for you to go. Follow Me. Keep your eyes open for the surprises I will surprise you with."

"From the ends of the earth I call to you, I call as
my heart grows faint; lead me to the
rock that is higher than I."
Psalm 61:2, NIV

Lifted Above Trouble

"I am here in the midst of you. I am the mighty one who saves. I am He who gives you the courage to be brave. I am the strength when you feel you are weak. I am the answer you find when you choose to seek. I give you solutions that you have never thought of. That is the beauty of allowing Me entrance into your heart and life. I lift you up and give you hope in the midst of strife. I am He who draws you near. I am He who makes the answer clear. You do not have to wander in wonder any longer. I will make clear the path I have laid before you. Trust Me to lead you forward into the unknown. You are the seed I have planted; My, how you have grown."

*"But he said to me, "My grace is sufficient for
you, for my power is made perfect in weakness."
Therefore I will boast all the more gladly about
my weaknesses, so that Christ's power
may rest on me."*
2 Corinthians 12:9, NIV

Power of Grace

"I have given you My grace. It is sufficient. I have given you the power you need to do what I have called you to do. Do not look at the outcome, perceived as it may be. I know the end from the beginning. Stay in the present, recognize My presence, and look to Me. I am calling you forth. I am giving you your next step. Take the step I have revealed to you, and you will see the next. Trust that I know the way. Trust that if you stray, you can get back on track by returning your gaze to Me. You were born for adventure. You are My work of art. I have loved you from the beginning. I have loved you from the very start."

"Arise, shine, for your light has come, and the glory of the Lord rises upon you."
Isaiah 60:1, NIV

Project the Light Within

"Speak My word and allow My light to shine forth from within you. I have given you solutions. I am He who creates the seen from that which was unseen. Follow My pattern and learn of My ways. I have put My Spirit in you to help you. You do not move forward alone. I go before you, with you and after you. I prepare and show you the way. Trust Me to guide you with My eye upon you. Look to Me and see where I am leading. I am your advocate. I am your defense. I am clarity in the midst of confusion. I am He who sees and answers your need. I am calling you forth into more of Me. Will you let Me lead you?"

*"Whoever serves me must follow me; and where
I am, my servant also will be. My Father will
honor the one who serves me."*
John 12:26, NIV

Follow Where I am

"I am the one with the heart to bless. I am the God of more not less. I am He who causes you to hear and see what I have prepared for you. Get ready to receive. Open hearts must first believe. Believe that I am for you, not against you. I am the one who helps you in your time of need. I am the one inviting you into the dance. I am asking you to join Me in the adventurous story of us. There are twists and turns along the way. Still, know that it is I who will always stay. I am by your side, through thick or thin. I am knocking on the door of your heart. Will you let Me in? Watch and see what I will do. Come boldly to Me and ask what you need. Confident in your position in Me. I am the one who is leading you forth. I have created the plan and chartered the course. Trust and follow. See where I lead. I am the answer to every need."

"The Lord said to me, "You have seen correctly,
for I am watching to see that my
word is fulfilled."
Jeremiah 1:12, NIV

Watch My Word

"You have sought Me and found Me. I am not hidden to not be found. I love when you search for Me. To watch your inquisitive eyes span the perimeter. Oh the look of joy on your face when you see I am there in your midst. I have always been here, and always will be. You can trust and rely on Me. I will not leave you. That is a promise you can take to the bank. I go before you and prepare the way. I go with you along the journey forward. I am behind you encouraging you when you are tired, and looking out for you. I see for you the whole picture of promise. You only see a piece. My word shall come to pass. Though it may tarry, wait for it. My word made flesh has come upon the scene to dwell in the midst of each of you. We dwell in the midst of each other. I am hidden in you, and you are hidden in Me. You are surrounded by My love and grace. I am the light others see on your face. I know the end from the beginning. Trust that I am for you. Together, let us move forth."

*"And we all, who with unveiled faces contemplate
the Lord's glory, are being transformed into his
image with ever-increasing glory, which comes
from the Lord, who is the Spirit."*
2 Corinthians 3:18, NIV

Power of Transformation

"I have filled you with favor and endued you with power. I
am near you this very hour. I have given you gifts for the
glorification of My name. Share with others, that you and they
may never be the same. I have called you to transformation
for transformation. I have filled you with My light so you can
lighten the dark places of others. Light is needed in times of
doubt. Scarcity flees when abundance is noticed. Notice where
I have already blessed you. You are well taken care of, My Love.
Forever and always, My Beloved you will be. Take My hand and
fellowship with Me. I call you in unity for the sake of our union.
There is a power and strength in togetherness."

"But thanks be to God, who always leads us as captives in Christ's triumphal procession and uses us to spread the aroma of the knowledge of him everywhere."
2 Corinthians 2:14, NIV

Victory Triumphs

"Fix your eyes on Me and you will begin to see. See that I am for you, not against you. You will see Me at work in your life. I am with you in triumph and strife. I have given you a peace that surpasses understanding. I have given you a joy unspeakable and full of glory. My glory shines on you. You are lifted up in faith when you feel weighed down in despair. I am He who knows your heart. I am He who hears your prayer. I am the one who brings you answers and solutions to problems that seemed unsolvable. I am He who has triumphed. I am the God of the possible. I am the one who declares My word and watches over that word to perform it. I watch over My word to see that it comes to pass. Partner with Me and watch how I will do wonders among you. My name is Faithful and True."

"...but few things are needed—or indeed only one.
Mary has chosen what is better, and it will not
be taken away from her."
Luke 10:42, NIV

Sit in the Stillness of Me

"Linger in My presence and be permeated in My love. I am with you always. As you look upon Me and know Me and My ways, you will begin to see how I've been working on your behalf. You are not forgotten, after all. You are very much remembered and very much loved. I will cause you to see more of Me the more time we spend together. You will know that I have given you gifts to be shared. Share them even if they may not be perfect. Rest assured, they are what others need. Do not let the fear of perfection or rejections keep you from My best for you. It is your obedience that speaks volumes of your love for Me. Obedience is born, not from obligation, but from love. It is love that clears away confusion and makes room for clarity. I am love and I am bringing clarity that drives out confusion. Walk forth this day in confidence, knowing that you do not go alone. Your gifts have a purpose: to bring light and life and hope."

*"Cast your cares on the Lord and he will sustain
you; he will never let the righteous be shaken."*
Psalm 55:22, NIV

Care for Our Concerns

"I have given you the best of Me. Will you give Me the rest of
you? Will you trust and see what I will do? I have your back.
There is no need to worry of lack. What is Mine is yours. You
always have access to more than you need. Trust in My word.
Plant your seed. I care about what concerns you. My ears are
always open and ready to listen to whatever you want to share.
I am never too busy and your concerns are never too small or
too big for Me to listen. I will provide you with the answers and
solutions you have not thought of. I see from a different vantage
point. You do well to seek wisdom from Me. When I give, I
give liberally. I spare no expense. You are My treasure. I want
for you, only the best. Trust that as you ask for direction, I give
it. Trust that when I give direction, you hear it. I reveal Myself
to you in new and exciting ways. I am from before time. I am
the Ancient of Days. Take time in your present to focus on My
presence. I am with you always."

*"Therefore I tell you, whatever you ask for in
prayer, believe that you have received it,
and it will be yours."*
Mark 11:24, NIV

Dare to Ask

"I will lead you and guide you in the way of truth. You will know the truth you seek. It shall refute the lies that have held you bound. Freedom is a choice away. It is found in knowing Me. When you know My character, you will know when something isn't of Me. Trust that I trust you. Trust that I speak to you and that you can hear Me. You are free to ask for that which you would not dare. I am expanding your boundaries so you have the courage to ask for the seemingly impossible. It is possible with Me. When you ask Me, you speak forth the desires I have known you have held. I know you better than you know yourself. I want you to know Me and you better, so you can know others better. I am sending others to you that need what I have given you. Be open to sharing. You have benefit of them as well. I am your shield. You have no use for a shell."

"As the heavens are higher than the earth, so are my ways higher than your ways and my thoughts than your thoughts."
Isaiah 55:9, NIV

Higher Sights

"I watch over My word to perform it. My word stands the test of time. I will confirm My word to you. You will know that what I speak is true. My vision for you goes far beyond that which you can see. Come up higher and see from My vantage point. I am taking off the limitations of your imagination. You were created in My image. You have creativity in your DNA. Choose to believe and step out into the more I have for you. Stir yourself up in your most holy faith and choose to declare My word over yourself, over your situations. What is it that I have said? What is the truth that you can rise up and declare? I am the one beyond compare. I am He who goes before you and shows you the way. I am the truth you speak. Come and let us create masterpieces together!"

"In the same way, let your light shine before others, that they may see your good deeds and glorify your Father in heaven."
Matthew 5:16, NIV

City on a Hill

"You are hidden in Me to be revealed by Me. Do not fear. It is not you they see, but Me. You are the platform from which My words can be shared. Others need to hear what I have placed upon your heart. I am a creative God and I am creating still. You are My creative one and you are creating still. Ask of Me to give you ideas and I will. Expand your thinking to receive the more I have for you. I have more for you than you can imagine. Invite Me into your day and watch how I show up. I am concerned with what concerns you. I have given you a hope. I am the hope that does not disappoint. You are the hope that does not disappoint Me. I have chosen to love you before you began. My love has not changed. Everlasting and unconditional are still the ways I love you. Receive the truth of My love and so let it transform you from the inside out. I am He who dispels your doubt."

"But remember the Lord your God, for it is he who gives you the ability to produce wealth, and so confirms his covenant, which he swore to your ancestors, as it is today."
Deuteronomy 8:18, NIV

Designed to Prosper

"In the silence, you will hear Me speak. I see you as strong, not weak. You are capable and called to do mighty exploits done in excellence. If it were not possible, I would not have said so. You do not go alone. I am working closely beside you and I have called others alongside you, as well. You will know those I have called by the heartbeats you share. Your heart beats for Me and My kingdom beyond compare. I am He who knows you intimately. I hear every request and I have counted every hair. You are the one I have chosen to do wonders. Believe you are worthy, because you are. You are Mine and that is all the proof you need. Take courage and plant the seed."

The King's Riches ©2017

"From the west, people will fear the name of the Lord, and from the rising of the sun, they will revere his glory. For he will come like a pent-up flood that the breath of the Lord drives along."
Isaiah 59:19, NIV

Victory Assured

"I fill your eyes with wonder. I fill your days with hope. I am on the scene. I am bringing you into the serene. I am your Peace when you have known only turmoil. My plans for you are good. They cannot be easily foiled. Trust Me to lead you, My upright one, on the path marked straight that I have laid out for you. I have created for you a highway to travel on. I have expanded your territory and given you firm ground to walk on. Trust that the way is safe for you to cross. It may look perilous, but know that I have gone before. You can do more than you thought capable of; so much more. I am filling the sails of your ship with the wind of My Spirit. You are meant to cover much ground. You are My adventure. You are the treasure I have found."

*"You will be a crown of splendor in the Lord's
hand, a royal diadem in the hand of your God."*
Isaiah 62:3, NIV

Reign with a Royal Crown

"I have rent the heavens and come down. I have placed upon
you a royal crown. I have given you authority to rule like the
royal one you are. It is not who you are or what you have done
that has qualified you. You are counted worthy simply because
you are Mine. You are Mine and you were born to shine. See
you as I see you. Look through the mirror of My eyes. I guide
you with My eye upon you. There is wisdom and direction
found in Me. Ask of Me and I will show you. You are Mine and
you have the ability to discern My voice from among those in
the crowd. Just as you are able to discern your own child's cry,
know that you can hear Me. I long to communicate with you; it
is one of My favorite things. Hearing your heart and being able
to speak wisdom, direction, and blessing. Seek Me and you will
find Me. I am the treasure you have sought after. You are the
treasure I have sought after. Yes, I have been looking for you.
There is much greatness in you that you have not seen yet. Stick
with Me and watch the wonder of you unfold. I am in the midst
of you and I am calling you forth into the more I have for you.
Do not look at doubt. Look at Me. I am hope personified."

*"I no longer call you servants, because a servant
does not know his master's business. Instead,
I have called you friends, for everything that I
learned from My Father I have made
known to you."*
John 15:15, NIV

Secrets with a Friend

"I have shown you the goodness of Me time and time again. I will continue to reveal Myself to you. I share with you much, because I call you friend. You will know what I am doing and you will see Me at work in your everyday. I am He who causes you to see and experience the extraordinary! You are the one I have chosen to do mighty exploits for Me. Do not ask Me to choose someone else. I have chosen you. I trust you to do that which I have laid on your heart to do. You do not accomplish this on your own. My Spirit dwells in you to help and guide you. I have given you seed to sow and I present you with opportunities to grow. Trust that I know what I am doing, even if you cannot see the outcome; especially when you cannot see the outcome. I can be trusted regardless. I am the hope that does not disappoint, the love that never fails, and the joy unspeakable and full of glory. You play a primary and essential role in the playing of your story."

"For God is not a God of disorder but of peace..."
1 Corinthians 14:33a, NIV

Clarity of the King

"I have given you the gift that keeps on giving: Me. I am the one who gifts you with creative ideas and solutions to problems you previously could not see a solution for. I am the way. I am the door. I am the one who goes before. I reveal Myself to you when you ask Me. I am speaking to you in many ways. I am He who was before time. I am the Ancient of Days. Confusion is not the protocol of My kingdom. I bring you clarity so you can increase in courage and confidence. I am leading you in a dance. You will cover much ground with Me as your leader. I guide you with My eye upon you. I have lifted you out of the pit and set your feet on solid rock. You are free to move forward in Me."

*"Enlarge the place of your tent, stretch your tent
curtains wide, do not hold back; lengthen your
cords, strengthen your stakes."*
Isaiah 54:2, NIV

Ready for Expansion

"You have more than you need to give to those I will show you.
Trust that I will not ask you to give something you do not have.
I am stretching you to expand your thinking, so I can bless you
even more. It is the open channel that water flows through. I
am a creative God and you are My creative one. I fashioned you
in My image and I have given you what you need and more.
When you do not know the way, ask Me to show you the open
door. I am the author of clarity, not confusion. I am the light. I
am faithful to reveal Myself to you, as you are obedient to ask.
You are the right one for the task. Trust that I see more in you
than you do. I call you forth as I see you. Not as others have
said you are. I am the bright and morning star. You are the one
I am calling forth to show others Me. I delight Myself in you.
I love to watch you step out and embrace your freedom! It is
for you! You are not forgotten. You are very much loved and
remembered."

"The thief comes only to steal and kill and
destroy; I have come that they may have life,
and have it to the full."
John 10:10, NIV

Life Lived to the Full

"I have come that you may have life to the full. You were not born for small thinking. I have placed My Spirit in you and have given you the power you need to accomplish the plans and purposes I have designed for you from before time began. You were on My heart and in My mind for forever and a day. I was with you then and forever I will stay. I have given you gifts that are uniquely yours to receive and use. Share what I have given with whom I will show you, and in the ways I will reveal to you. You are more than what you have been. Think broader. Expand your mind and heart to receive the more I have for you. My greatness is within you. It is My greatness that will rise forth, as you rise up in Me. Get ready. I am not done creating with you. There is more to do."

"For all those who exalt themselves will be humbled, and those who humble themselves will be exalted."
Luke 14:11, NIV

The Humble Exalted

"You shine with My glory to reveal My glory to others. Others see Me in you. You are My ambassador. You are My representative in your day to day. You go about doing ordinary tasks with extraordinary ramifications. The weight of My glory has arisen upon you and I have called you My own for My plans and purposes. With great power comes great responsibility. I have chosen you as able for the task. There is greatness in you that I see and others see. As you walk in My obedience, you will see the greatness in you as well. Your heart is humble and teachable to Me. This is why I have chosen you. Trust My decision and trust My process. I know what I am doing always and in all ways. You are My example and I have made you in excellence. You are not the exception to the rule. That which I have done for others, I will do for you, too."

*"Let us not become weary in doing good, for at
the proper time we will reap a harvest if
we do not give up."*
Galatians 6:9, NIV

Due Season

"I have given you a resiliency and an ability to persist until you
have seen My promise fulfilled. You know that I am a God of
My word. My word will accomplish what I have called you to
do. Grow forward with Me and see you as I see you. I see you as
the original design I have created you to be. You will know the
truth that sets you free. No longer are you bound to looking on
the ground. I am your glory and the lifter of your head! Look
into My eyes of love and see yourself in their reflection. Yes, it
is you that I desire. It is you I have such hope and joy and love
for. I have given you the moon and so much more. Ask of Me
what you desire. Ask Me to expand your mind and heart so it
can receive the more of Me I long to give. Embrace that which
I have for you. Believe it is for you. I have not left you, nor have
I forgotten. I am here, forever and always. I am the hope that
stays."

*"If you believe, you will receive whatever
you ask for in prayer."*
Matthew 21:22, NIV

Believe for the Answer

"I am the solution you seek. Asking Me does not make you weak. When you ask, believe I will answer. I will come through for you in ways you could not imagine. I am a creative God and I still create today. I will give you creative ideas and solutions if you ask. We are partners together, you and I. Whatever you have need of, I am your supply. My love is a well so deep it never runs dry. I am concerned with what concerns you. Before you ask, I answer. While you are still speaking, I hear. I am not as far as you would suppose. In fact, I am quite near. I have given you a reason to rejoice. Speak forth My word. Let Me hear your voice. There is a power in My word that cannot be denied. Come into the light. You do not have to hide. I see you and I hear; rest assured, I am near."

*"Therefore, since we are surrounded by such
a great cloud of witnesses, let us throw off
everything that hinders and the sin that so easily
entangles. And let us run with perseverance
the race marked out for us,"*
Hebrews 12:1, NIV

Lay Aside the Weight

"You have let go of that which does not serve you. You are well on your way in embracing your freedom. I will reveal more of Myself to you if you ask. In so doing, I will show you old mindsets and beliefs that have held you back. No longer will you live in fear of lack. I am the one who provides for your needs. I always have and I always will. As you begin to believe in and step out in My truth, others will begin to do the same. Your freedom is not about you, it is about those you will impact and influence for My glory. Take heart, I know the rest of the story. It is good. You are good. I have chosen well when I chose you for Me. Celebrate the wins and revel in the victory!"

*"You will keep in perfect peace those whose minds
are steadfast, because they trust in you."*
Isaiah 26:3, NIV

Perfect Peace

"I have given you a hope that does not disappoint. I am the constant in a world of variables. Look to Me and gain your bearings. I am he who never lets go of you. I am by your side always. I go before you and show you the way. I lead you forward into the great unknown. There is nothing to fear when you know I am here. I reveal My plans and purposes to you. You will see Me at work in your life. I am calling you forward into peace and out of strife. Trust that I have the plan and I know the outcome. I have much for you to do. Worry is not one of them. Trust is the key to the serenity you seek. When you trust in My goodness you can rest in My grace. I am the light that shines on your face. The light of My love chases away the darkness of fear."

"...being confident of this, that he who began a good work in you will carry it on to completion until the day of Christ Jesus."
Philippians 1:6, NIV

Faithful to Complete

"I have begun a good work in you and I will complete it. I will not leave you unfinished. You are My work of art that I am proud to sign and display for others to see. You, My dear, glorify Me. Others look at the light of your face and notice Me in you. You shine brighter than you realize. Others take notice of you because they see Me in you. Embrace that favor I have esteemed you with. Share what I have given you with those I will show you. Others have need of what you have to share. Each of you is unique and beyond compare. I am your compass. I am your plumb line. I am calling you to participate in love divine. You will know the etiquette and protocol of My kingdom. As you lean in and learn from Me, you will realize a freedom you have never seen. It is for you; for your betterment and enjoyment. I see the best in you and I call it forth. Embrace your uniqueness. Recognize your worth."

*"Therefore, the promise comes by faith, so that
it may be by grace and may be guaranteed to
all Abraham's offspring—not only to those who
are of the law but also to those who have the
faith of Abraham. He is the father of us all. As
it is written: "I have made you a father of many
nations." He is our father in the sight of God, in
whom he believed—the God who gives life to the
dead and calls into being things that were not."*
Romans 4:1-17, NIV

Called Forth

"I have given you My peace. There is no need to leave a fleece.
I am true to My word. What I said I will do, rest assured, I will
do. If you need confirmation I will gladly give it. But know that
it must then lead to action. You cannot just sit on confirmation.
You have a role to play in the fulfilling of My plans for you. I
will lead, but you must follow. I am calling you forth into My
best for you. I have not forgotten you. You have always been in
My mind and on My heart. I call you forth by the completed
work I see in you. If you have trouble believing you are as I
see you, ask Me to show you how to see better and to think
differently. I delight when you come to Me with your questions,
fears and concerns. I have freed you so you can help others
become free themselves. No lesson is ever wasted. Taste and
see that I am good. Savor the favor that is yours in Me. Delight
yourself in My love so free."

"Let his faithful people rejoice in this honor and sing for joy on their beds."
Psalm 149:5, NIV

Releasing Joy

"I am inviting you into the fun that is found in Me. I have loosed your chains and you are free. I have it all planned out. Rejoice this day! Smile and lift up a shout. There is a freedom and power in the releasing and reveling in joy. I am He who causes you to laugh. You are so beautiful when you are enjoying the gifts I have given you. The way your eyes smile when you take in the sunrise. The lilt in your laughter when I catch you by surprise! My words are the truth that destroys the lies. Ask Me to show you where I am at work in your life. You will see and know that I am here. I am for you. I am your advocate, your protector and King. Release your joy and let freedom ring."

"If any of you lacks wisdom, you should ask God,
who gives generously to all without finding
fault, and it will be given to you."
James 1:5, NIV

Wisdom Shared

"I have given you wisdom just like you have asked. I will not deny My best from you. I am He who loves to lavish My best for you. No good thing will I withhold from you who walks in right relationship with Me. Trust that I will both protect and provide for you. Do not strive to figure out the details that I will provide. Follow My lead. Walk in peace and not in fear. You will know I am near. I care about that which concerns you. You are free to talk with Me about it. I am not too busy for you and your concerns are not too trivial for Me. Trust that you are cared for. You are loved beyond measure. You truly are My treasure. You are the one I fought for. You are worth it. I know the true value of who you are, and all you will do and be. You are favored by Me. Rest in the knowledge that I am for you. You are in My mind and on My heart; together forever and never to part."

"You have enlarged the nation and increased their joy; they rejoice before you as people rejoice at the harvest, as warriors rejoice when dividing the plunder. For as in the day of Midian's defeat, you have shattered the yoke that burdens them, the bar across their shoulders, the rod of their oppressor."
Isaiah 9:3-4, NIV

Unbounded Freedom

"Love is My litmus test. You will know others and others will know you by My love. I have broken the chains that have held you bound. There is power in My word to see that which was lost, found. No longer are you hidden in the shackles of fear, dread and doubt. You are free to explore that which I have planned for you. I am for you, not against you. I want for you the highest good. Trust My heart and My motives for you. It will cause you to fully embrace My gifts. I will take you places you have never been. You will do things you have never imagined. Follow My lead and see how Hope opens opportunities. You are more than what you have known before. I see you as you are, fully and complete. Embrace My future for you. Do not let the past compete. I have called you out of the ashes to arise in the beauty that has been within you all along. I am your hope. I am your home."

"The Spirit of the Sovereign Lord is on me,
because the Lord has anointed me to proclaim
good news to the poor. He has sent me to bind up
the brokenhearted, to proclaim freedom for the
captives and release from darkness
for the prisoner,"
Isaiah 61:1, NIV

Free to Set Others Free

"I am calling you forth to be a solution to many. You are not in the way. There is room for you and you are very much wanted. You are needed more than you know. You are not forgotten. You are remembered. You mean more to so much more than you can imagine. You think your gifts are inadequate, so you hesitate sharing them. Many miss out when you do not share what I have given you to share. Do not look at the size of your gift, whether it is too small or too large. Know this: it is just right. Share and grow in faith and confidence. You do not go alone. Your courage to share sets forth a domino effect for others to share. The time has come for the walls I have not built to come down. You are not meant to be hidden. You are not meant to be isolated. I have called you as part of a whole. Others see that you fill a need for them. Oh that you would see it too. You are a solution and I am setting you in place. Get ready for the more I have for you."

"See, I am doing a new thing! Now it springs up;
do you not perceive it? I am making a way in the
wilderness and streams in the wasteland."
Isaiah 43:19, NIV

Provision Provided

"I give you streams in the desert. I provide for you in all things and in all ways. I am the one who has your back. You need not ever live in a mindset of lack. I am He who protects you. I give My best for My best. I know what you need before you even ask. It is ok to ask. Asking does not mean you are greedy or ungrateful. Asking reveals to Me that you know who you are. You know whose you are. You trust Me to answer you because you know I hear. I am providing you solutions you have not thought of before. Do not be afraid to try the silly solutions. Logic does not always make the most sense. I have gifted you with a heart that is in tune with Me. Take the steps forth that I show you. I have not forgotten you. This is the day to go forth and see the land I have given you to inherit. It is yours!"

*"We have this hope as an anchor for the soul, firm
and secure. It enters the inner sanctuary
behind the curtain,"*
Hebrews 6:19, NIV

Anchored in Truth

"I have given you the wisdom you seek. The wisdom you have
asked for. You trust Me enough to ask Me. Trust Me enough
to answer you. I reveal Myself to you in ways that you know I
am speaking to you. As you begin to hear Me more and more,
you will know I am the door. I have granted you access to Me
at any time. You will know our life sublime. I have given you
strategies for success. As you see Me at work in your life a little,
you will see I have been there all along. I am your solution and
I cause you to be a solution to others. I have given you answers
to problems. Share them without fear. Simply because you
recognize that I am here. Anchor yourself in Me. Grasp the
truth that I have set you free. I have freed you to be who I have
called you to be. Tiny steps lead to giant leaps. The important
thing is consistent forward movement. I am the God of more. I
am the God of improvement."

"A generous person will prosper; whoever
refreshes others will be refreshed."
Proverbs 11:25, NIV

Generosity is Love in Action

"You carry the light others need. Share liberally to those I will show you who to share with. I have given you more than enough. The generous soul becomes rich. He who invests in others finds great reward in leaning into My leading. Humble yourself and learn of Me. I will take you places you have never been and show you things you have never seen. You hold within you the solutions others need. You are a key player and are very much valued. Others are not their fullest potential if you are not yours. Gain your inspiration from Me and share it forth. May there be no stopping the wildfire of the revolution of love that I, Myself, have started. Share My presence and so help to shape the futures of others. Follow where I lead and so plant the seed."

*"Whether you turn to the right or to the left, your
ears will hear a voice behind you, saying,
'This is the way; walk in it.'"*
Isaiah 30:21, NIV

The Way to Go

"I have given you the best part of Me. I only give the best for
My best. You are the one I have called. You are the one I give to
and receive from. Look to Me when you cannot find your way. I
will show you. I am He who is faithful and true. I do what I say
and I say what I do. I am the one who fashioned your plan. I go
with you as you possess your land. See and believe the plans I
have designed. Look and see who I have divinely aligned. You
are not alone. You are not left behind. You are free to be the you
I have called you to be. Embrace and rejoice in My land of the
free."

"But you are a chosen people, a royal priesthood,
a holy nation, God's special possession, that you
may declare the praises of him who called you
out of darkness into his wonderful light."
1 Peter 2:9, NIV

Proclaiming Praises

"Behold, I give you My glory for My glory. You shine brighter than you know. Trust My leading and go with My flow. I will tell you where to go. I am revealing Myself to you in ways which you cannot deny. I have heard your prayers and I will answer your cry. I give to you that which you need and more. I am the Way, the Truth and the Door. Enter into all that I have prepared for you in advanced. You are not an afterthought. You have been on My mind since before there was time. Believe that you are that cherished because it is true. There is only one original you. You are My treasure, My gift, the one I love."

*"You will seek me and find me when you
seek me with all your heart."*
Jeremiah 29:13, NIV

Seek and Find

"I will reveal to you the mysteries of Me. I see your searching heart and I will respond in ways that will astound. You, My love, are free. No longer are you bound. I have given you a holy curiosity in Me. Seek Me and find Me. Lean on Me and learn of My ways. Take what you learn and share it with another. Your growth produces growth in others. That is the beauty and legacy of learning. Keep learning. Keep growing. Keep loving. My faithfulness and love never end. Do not think you know it all. Be flexible and willing to bend. I have created you to seek Me out. Know that it is I who also seek you. You are no longer forsaken. You are sought after. You are not abandoned. You are very much wanted. I have given you gifts to share with others. Do so with a heart bent toward Me. Celebrate! This is the day you are free."

"Again, the kingdom of heaven is like a merchant looking for fine pearls. When he found one of great value, he went away and sold everything he had and bought it."
Matthew 13:45-46, NIV

Treasure of Great Price

"You are My prince. You are not a pauper. A poverty mentality does not suit the King's own child. I will show you your inheritance if you will look to Me. I guide you with My eye. Look to Me to see where you are going. I have never left your side and I never will. I am here beside you, leading you still. I will continue to reveal Myself to you in ways that will astound. I have loosed your chains. No longer are you bound. Rise up in victory and let your feet and heart dance. You are worth the chance! You are worth everything I paid for you and more. Enter into your inheritance. There is a place for you at the table. I have granted you access through Me, the Door. Enter into the freedom I have called you to. Do not doubt any longer. Know that the gifts I have given are for you. You are the treasure of My heart."

"In the Lord's hand the king's heart is a stream of water that he channels toward all who please him."
Proverbs 21:1, NIV

Appointed and Anointed

"I have marked you and anointed you for My plans and purposes. You are not without design. You are unequivocally Mine. I have given you all of Me. I have done so, willingly. You are the one who has captivated My heart. It is you. It has been you from the start. Take what I have given you and use it to bless another. Then, they in turn, will do the same. I have started the revolution. I am the cornerstone and capstone of the building of My people. Strengthen the bond you have with others; the stronger your connections, the deeper your bonds. I am the one who goes about seeking those hearts who are for Me. I seek and I find. Just as you seek and find Me. My heart is for you. I only want your best. Give out of a heart of love, and let Me handle the rest. You are the one who has moved My heart with love."

"I will send you rain in its season, and the ground
will yield its crops and the trees their fruit."
Leviticus 26:4, NIV

Rain in Due Season

"There is freedom in the boundaries of My love. You need not look outside of what you already have in Me. I will provide for you what you need. Trust Me. I have given you the seed. Ask Me where to sow and I will show you. I know where the seed will be the most fruitful. I see the soil of the hearts of men. Trust Me in the process of growing. You will yield a bountiful harvest. It is I that grows. You plant and trust. As you allow Me room to move in your heart and life, you will see exponential growth. You are beautiful to behold. As you behold Me more and more, the more My glory shines upon you. You reflect that which you have been gazing upon. Fix your focus on things that serve you well. Do not dwell on that which causes confusion, division and strife. You are meant for more. Do not settle for less than I have already provided and planned for you. You are My anointed one who brings Me much joy. You are perfumed with the fragrance of My presence. You impact nations for Me. Trust and see. Plant and it will grow."

*"Who dares despise the day of small things, since
the seven eyes of the Lord that range throughout
the earth will rejoice when they see the chosen
capstone in the hand of Zerubbabel?"*
Zechariah 4:10, NIV

Small Beginnings Have Great Potential

"I have given you what you need, what you have asked for. You think I have not because it is not in the way you expect. Just as I sent My Son as a baby, so I also do with your answers. Oftentimes answers and solutions will come in seed form. But you must not despise the day of small beginnings. Be at rest and know I am at work. I do hear, I do care and I do answer. Trust the process. Trust Me to deliver to you what I have promised. I am Faithful and True. What I say I will do, I will do. Make no mistake, I do not lie. I hear each laugh and I see each cry. I am more involved than you know. But I want you to know Me more fully. Know that I am a gentleman and not a bully. I will not force you to love, but I do draw you forth in hopes you will respond. No matter if you choose to engage or not. I love you still. I love you regardless. You are the joy in My heart and the reason for My happiness."

"I led them with cords of human kindness, with ties of love. To them I was like one who lifts a little child to the cheek, and I bent down to feed them."
Hosea 11:4, NIV

Drawn In By Love

"It is My kindness that leads you to repentance. My love produces a mindset shift that will open the way for you to experience the more I have for you. Believe that which I offer is yours. If you do not believe it belongs to you, how can you receive it? I am teaching you how to see you and others as I see you. As you think on Me more often, more often you will begin to think like Me. You become what you behold. You receive more of what you focus on. This is a principle that works whether you are aware of it or not. I am the one who leads you next to Me. I call you that we may explore your land together. The land I have laid out for you to possess. Do not be afraid of the giants, but be in awe of Me. Watch and see how I take care of My own. You are the one I call My home."

*"Very truly I tell you, unless a kernel of wheat
falls to the ground and dies, it remains
only a single seed. But if it dies, it
produces many seeds."*
John 12:24, NIV

Harvest Hidden in the Seed

"The very thought of you brings a smile to Me. I so enjoy our times together. We have so much fun! You bring much joy and laughter. Oh that you would see the value that you bring. Believe in the worth I see in you. You are beautiful to behold. You are not too young or too old. You are just right for the purposes and plans I have called you to do. Trust Me that I know what I am doing. You do not have to know all the answers. That is My job. Your job is to trust Me and follow My lead. I have given you a harvest that is hidden in the seed. Stay by Me and gather My instruction. Heed My words and get ready for celebration. Today is the day I have set before you. Choose to follow and be open to rejoice."

"...for though the righteous fall seven times,
they rise again,"
Proverbs 24:16a, NIV

Learning to Rise

"I have gifted you the gift of My power. I will teach you how to use it skillfully. So it is with all My gifts. Not only must they be used, they must be mastered by the skilled craftsmen that you are. This is not about perfection, but progression. You will grow in your gifts as you continually and consistently step out to use them. Be not afraid of making mistakes. They are opportunities to learn. Heed what you hear Me say. If you get it wrong, I am more than able to set you back in right standing. I am right by your side and I am right behind you. I teach you to use your gifts like teaching you to ride a bike. Sometimes I let you ride on your own, but you are never out of My reach. When you fall, I encourage you to try again. I know that one day you will get it , one day you will master the skill of bike riding. Trust Me that I know and see what you do not. That is why we need each other. No one person is the whole answer. Together we are a solution. Love is My revolution."

"Before they call I will answer; while they
are still speaking I will hear."
Isaiah 65:24, NIV

I Answer the Call

"I am concerned with what concerns you. Make no mistake. I care, I hear and I answer. I give you hope where you thought you could never find it. I give you love when it seemed to always allude you. I am the answer you have been seeking all this time. I am the reason behind your rhyme. I have given you the skills to move to the beat of My heart. My heart beats in sync with your steps in Me. Together we move as one. Together we will celebrate the victory won. I am He who causes your heart to stir. You will know the more that you long for. It is found in Me. It always has been and always will be. I encourage you forth to have increasing encounters with Me. Walk in your victory. Dance in your freedom. It is I who calls you forth. It is I who bids you come. Live in the light of My love. The light that shines on your face is evidence of My amazing grace."

*"Like apples of gold in settings of silver is
a ruling rightly given."*
Proverbs 29:11, NIV

Right Words at the Right Time

"I have known you before the beginning of time. I have called you and you are Mine. Behold, you are wanted and cherished and chosen. My love thaws the hearts so frozen. I have begun a great work in you and I will complete it. Know that you do have a place. There is a role that you perfectly fit. I will lead you to others and lead others to you. You will know where you belong. I give you words to your own song. I have written you on the door of My heart. Together we are one, never to part. I have gifted you with gifts that are uniquely yours. Steward and share them well. For of your gifts, My love does tell. Others see Me in their everyday life. Your words fitly spoken, relieves them in strife. Speak forth the words you hear Me say. Take someone's night and show them the light of day. You can do what I am calling you. Believe it to be true. Know you do not go alone. My power in you, yielded to Me, brings light to the blind and sets the bound free."

"So do not fear, for I am with you; do not be dismayed, for I am your God. I will strengthen you and help you; I will uphold you with my righteous right hand."
Isaiah 41:10, NIV

Secured in the Arms of Love

"Love will not loose its hold on you. I have you securely in My arms. The grip with which you hold Me is entirely your choice. You are free to choose. That is the beauty of My love for you. It is both given and received freely. I am as close to you as you are comfortable with Me being. I am a true gentleman at heart and will not push beyond the boundaries you have placed. Still I desire to know you more. Still I reveal Myself to you in ways that you will know it is Me who speak to you. I am the one with you always. There is never a need to fear when I am here. There is also never a dull moment. I call you forth on a grand adventure. Will you join Me?"

"The blessing of the Lord brings wealth,
without painful toil for it."
Proverbs 10:22, NIV

Blessings of His Benefits

"I have given you the gift of opportunity. Daily I load you with benefits and give you opportunities to be a blessing to others. Be the Me that they see in you and shine brightly. Nothing will I withhold from those who walk uprightly. As you are transparently you, you allow the light of Me to shine through you. I have given you what you think you lack. It is already yours. I always have your back. Look and see and look and see again. You will see wonders done among you that will make you look twice. That is the goodness of My love and evidence of how much I love you!"

"You hem me in behind and before, and
you lay your hand upon me."
Psalm 139:5, NIV

The Light that Travels

"You are My beloved one, in whom I am well pleased. It is nothing you have done. It is simply whose you are. You are Mine and you are loved. My love is a gift, that when received, grows. So it is with all My gifts. As you receive them and make them your own, they grow. Your capacity for more grows and you continue to listen and obey. You will see your night turned to day because I am the light that travels. I go where you go. I go before you and I show you the way. Gather your courage and seize the day. My commands are not burdensome because we partner together. I am the joy in the midst of your journey. I am the one who fills you with hope that will flush out the doubt if you let it. It is up to you. It is the way I designed it to be. I chose you. You are free to not choose Me. The choice is yours. It is a continual choice. I am the one who gives you a voice."

"Accept one another, then, just as Christ accepted you, in order to bring praise to God."
Romans 15:7, NIV

Accepted in Him

"I have given you more than you think you need. Trust that I have given you the seed. I will show you how and where and when to sow. I will guide you with My eye and lead you where to go. I am the one who goes before you and prepares the way. Trust that you hear My voice. You are Mine and I speak to My own. You are the one I have called My home. I have found My dwelling place with you. I have counted you worthy. That is enough. You do not have to perform for Me. I have accepted you from the beginning. I have not changed My mind about you. I love you altogether perfectly. No matter what you have done or have not done. My love is unconditional. My love is eternal."

*"Those who look to him are radiant; their faces
are never covered with shame."*
Psalm 34:5, NIV

Radiant One

"I have called you for greatness. No, I have not made a mistake in calling you. I see in you what you do not yet see. I see you as whole and completely free. I see the end from the beginning and I call it forth. The working it out is not automatic. There is a role you must play in your own freedom. I will show you the steps to move forward. Look to Me and you will notice your chains are free. They no longer hold you bound by fear and lack and despair. I know your story. I know you from the inside out. You quicken My heart and with love, I shout. I am causing you to see you as I see you. Let Me be your mirror. Trust what I show you. You are beautiful and radiant! That is the truth of your story. Engage in the adventure. You were made for the epic."

"Fear the Lord, you his holy people, for those
who fear him lack nothing."
Psalm 34:9, NIV

Provision Prevails

"I have come to give you more; more of Me. I have given you all of Me. I hold nothing back. You are abundantly free. With Me, there is no lack. If you cannot see the table I have prepared for you, ask Me to show you. You will see Me at work in the midst of your life. I am the calm in the midst of strife. I am always here. I am never too far. I am with you wherever you are. I empower you to empower others; to see the tools I have given. Come to Me and I will show you how to use your gifts with skill and precision. I supply you with both vision and provision. I will show you who you are to be aligned with to bring about the vision I have given. It cannot be done alone. I have given you a family to call home. Trust Me even when you cannot see the final picture. You are an important part of the masterpiece I am creating. I am from forever to forever. I created then and I am creating still."

*"This is what the Lord says: 'Let not the wise
boast of their wisdom or the strong boast of their
strength or the rich boast of their riches, but let
the one who boasts boast about this: that they
have the understanding to know me, that I am
the Lord, who exercises kindness, justice and
righteousness on earth, for in these
I delight,' declares the Lord."*
Jeremiah 9:23-24, NIV

Glory of Knowing Wisdom and Worth

"I have given you the wisdom you seek. I exalt the humble.
Those who recognize their need for Me are those who will taste
the sweetness of freedom. I release them from their chains of
doubt and despair. They shall know that I care. I care and you
matter. You matter more than you think you do. I am not too
busy and your requests are never too big or too small. Dare
to ask, to seek and to find. You will know you are one of a
kind. There is no one else quite like you. You are a one-and-
only original. There is a role that only you can fill. Receive the
weightiness of My truth. You ask Me if you are worthy of love.
Look in the mirror and see the living breathing proof. My
answer is a resounding yes. I love you perfectly and for always.
You have never left My gaze."

"The fear of the Lord is pure, enduring forever.
The decrees of the Lord are firm, and all of them
are righteous. They are more precious than gold,
than much pure gold; they are sweeter than
honey, than honey from the honeycomb."
Psalm 19:9-10, NIV

True Treasure of Worth

"I have proven your worth. As gold is tested in fire and proved of great value, so I have tested you and proven your value. You are more precious to Me than you know. Allow Me room to show. Allow Me space in your heart and life so I can be free to be Me with you. I will show you how precious you are and I will open your eyes to see and believe if you are willing to look. You cannot see the beauty that is before you in the mirror, if you do not stop and look. Take a step back to assess, so you can grow forward in Me. Slow down and savor the goodness of Me. Taste the flavor in the gift of each day. Come alongside Me and let us celebrate and conquer the day! I have much to show you. Lace up your boots and lasso the day! Adventure is calling and I know the way."

Author Information

Tamarah hails from the great state of Ohio. From a very young age, she has sought opportunities to encourage others, and she delights in seeing others smile. Tamarah is passionate about seeking what the Lord is speaking and sharing what she hears with others. She is an avid lover of music and movies, and also enjoys discovering new trails in nature and in life. Feel free to contact Tamarah at tamarahwest8@gmail.com

Made in the USA
Columbia, SC
09 July 2017